D0723918

Acclaim for Supply Chain Save

An AMR Research Publication

"AMR Research's work on the global supply chain is driving change in business and is something from which leading companies can certainly benefit. Equally interesting is how the book demonstrates the way this relatively new discipline is being used to solve world problems."

—Stu Reed, Executive Vice President,
Integrated Supply Chain, Motorola, Inc.

"AMR Research describes a new way of doing business, a new model that IBM calls the globally integrated enterprise. And fundamentally, it all starts with the supply chain, which can be the catalyst to integrate operations and production to deliver value to clients worldwide."

—Bob Moffat, Senior Vice President,
Integrated Operations, IBM Corporation

"An innovative book showing how supply chain concepts can help both companies and society grapple with the challenges of globalization, environmental sustainability, and world health. Supply chain management has come a long way!"

—Warren H. Hausman, Department of
Management Science and Engineering,
Stanford University

Supply Chain
Saves the World

Supply Chain
Saves the World

Series Editor
Bruce Richardson

Edition Editor
Kevin O'Marah

Editor
Randy Weston

AMR Research

Copyright 2006 by AMR Research, Inc.
An AMR Research Publication
All rights reserved
AMR Research® is a registered trademark of AMR Research, Inc.

No portion of this publication may be reproduced in whole or in part without
the prior written permission of AMR Research. Any written materials are protected by United States copyright laws and international treaty provisions. AMR
Research is not a registered investment advisor, and it is not the intent of this
book to recommend specific companies for investment, acquisition, or other
financial considerations.

To request permission to use parts of this book or order copies, contact the director
of publications at bookreprints@amrresearch.com, or write to AMR Research, 125
Summer Street, Fourth Floor, Boston MA 02110-1616. Telephone: 617.542.6600,
8:30 a.m. to 5:30 p.m. ET, Monday through Friday. Fax: 617.542.5670.

Library of Congress Data
Supply chain saves the world.
    Includes index.
    ISBN 0-9785928-0-8

                                                          2006926583
                                                          LCCN

Second printing, November 2006
Printed in the United States of America
10 9 8 7 6 5 4 3 2

This book is printed on 100% post-consumer recycled fiber. It is manufactured
entirely with wind-generated electricity and in accordance with a Forest Stewardship
Council (FSC) pilot program that certifies products made with high percentages of
post-consumer reclaimed materials.

Table of Contents

Risk Management: The Supply Chain Responds

The Practitioner's Guide

Preface

Making money and saving the world at the same time: the supply chain revolution is making all of this possible— and profitable.

Solving world hunger. This phrase is commonly used to signify an impossible task. Yet for many supply chain professionals, the fusion of global engineering, manufacturing, and logistics with Internet-enabled information technology presents, for the first time in history, a real chance to actually solve world hunger.

The worldwide network of manufacturers and retailers that deliver food, medicine, and machines to serve humankind are fast developing a new, demand-driven model of managing the global supply chain. New depths of visibility into the needs of consumers are increasingly matched by a richer understanding of the abilities of business to meet those needs profitably. No longer do grimy factories push cookie-cutter products to customers. Demand-driven supply networks sense and respond to real-time demands across a network of suppliers to match capability with opportunity.

The real engine of change remains the quest of business for sustainable profits. In the search for new growth markets, big business is seeing opportunity in the complex problems that face the world. Developing-world demand for consumer products and the infrastructure to deliver them offer huge potential for those able to serve these markets. Developed-world requirements for environmental sustainability, wider access to healthcare, and disaster response similarly present new business opportunities to those equipped to innovate their products and processes. In chasing these opportunities for shareholder benefit, global companies can improve human welfare.

In *Supply Chain Saves the World*, AMR Research assembles research carried out over several years into the mechanics of the supply chain revolution that is making all of this possible. We have been working with manufacturers and retailers for 20 years to study how information technology is applied to business and the supply chain. In this time we have seen our clients wrestle with issues like globalization, environmental compliance, and risk management in their business and supply chain strategies. We have broken down the process and technology components of these strategies to understand where and how investment makes sense. This book presents this research at a strategic and practitioner level.

Chapter 1 sets a historical context for the development of this demand-driven model while raising the debate to link business performance at the highest level with the welfare of humankind. The ideal of today's supply chain is agility so that cash invested in operations yields quick returns, but without sacrificing liquidity. As such, 21st-century supply chains are no longer about matching supply with demand, but capability with opportunity. Chapter 1 also provides an organizational model for companies striving to become more demand driven and identifies those leaders—AMR Research's Supply Chain Top 25—that best exemplify its practice.

In Chapter 2, we explore the topic of globalization in the supply chain. As global markets come to mean customers as well as suppliers, opportunity abounds. Familiar habits, however, break down when new partners are engaged for sourcing, engineering and design, and distribution. Similarly, longstanding assumptions about the rule of law, intellectual property, and market development are proving false in many new markets. We address these issues in this chapter by describing how to organize for global markets, how to tap developing world talent, and what pitfalls to watch for in the most competitive emerging market, China.

Chapter 3 focuses supply chain discipline on the problem of environmental sustainability. At one level, business needs to comply with the surging set of new regulations. Preparedness for these regulations is essential, but unfortunately more complex than many organizations realize. As a business opportunity, however, the push toward green products and supply chains offers payback for those who take the lead. Active compliance means using green regulations and consumer sentiment as a competitive advantage. Businesses ranging from basic chemicals and electronics through grocery and fashion retail will find this chapter helpful in terms of specific compliance direction and branding for differentiation.

Healthcare presents a tremendous challenge, both to rich countries that spend as much as 10 percent of GDP on the sector and to developing nations, which face severe shortages of everything from drugs to hospital beds. Productivity gains seen in other industries suggest real potential for similar gains in healthcare. In Chapter 4, we get into supply chain disciplines, including faster new drug development and better epidemic response mechanisms. Lessons can be taken from the demand-driven model evolving in other industries to improve healthcare delivery and basic human welfare.

Chapter 5 is about risk management strategies in the interdependent global supply network. As discussed in Chapter 2, globalization presents opportunity and risk to business. A spate of natural and manmade disasters the past few years has illustrated how important the risk half of this equation has become. Supply chain serves business by managing risk to limit the cost of disruptions. In terms of human welfare, the quick response of supply chains to Hurricane Katrina demonstrates how such abilities help society at large. This chapter identifies best practices in supply chain risk management and details specific risk management strategies that companies are using today.

Whether the goal is grand or mundane, the lives of supply chain practitioners have become dramatically more complex. Constantly weighing business tradeoffs calls for a set of tools and techniques that they can rely on as their organizations continue to raise the bar. Chapter 6 summarizes several practical tools AMR Research has developed or uncovered the past 20 years. We explore five basic demand-driven strategies and break down the vital concept of supply chain agility. We end by detailing our supply chain benchmarking toolset, with definitions of critical performance metrics and enablers.

Supply Chain Saves the World is designed to provide supply chain professionals with a sense of mission and with tactical advice to use in the real world. Although the material represents a comprehensive body of research, we have structured the book to allow readers to select individual chapters without depending on previous ones for context.

We look forward to sharing our excitement about the opportunity for supply chain and technology professionals to make a difference for their companies—and for the world.

Kevin O'Marah
May 2006

Introduction

Winning businesses will be the heroes of the next decade. I'm not talking about celebrity CEOs—I'm talking about the quietly competent practitioners who will dominate the global supply chain to meet demand whenever and wherever it exists. They will be the heroes because, as global business further develops, it will be in the interest of these winning businesses to solve global problems.

In fact, it is the ability of these companies to address these problems as supply chain leaders that will distinguish them from their competitors. A stretch? Maybe. But it's no coincidence that supply chain leaders like Wal-Mart, Home Depot, and Procter & Gamble, each featured in the AMR Research Supply Chain Top 25 for 2005, were among the first to meet the needs of the victims of Hurricane Katrina.

Global opportunity breeds social responsibility

Most companies now rely more on partners from every region of the world to bring new products to market and fulfill demand. As a result, the basis of competition in industry has shifted to how effectively a company manages its global supply network.

This new reality will force the best corporate leaders to also be great corporate citizens because, amid these globalization trends, the winners will be those that can manage both sides of a paradox of conflicting goals:

- Governments rely on us for their economic well being but increasingly impose regulations on us to protect the communities in which we operate.

- A global supply base allows us to get to market faster and at a lower cost, but our dependence on this base leaves our businesses more affected by the global issues that could impede commerce. As a result, the best are ready to respond to the unexpected, be they natural disasters like the tsunami in Southeast Asia, the potential for rapidly spreading disease like SARS or the avian flu, or the effect of warfare, terrorism, port strikes, or other people-led events.

- The global demand for goods and services offers unprecedented opportunity, but it's also causing a shortage of available natural resources as well as human capital.

- We benefit as a growing percentage of the world industrializes, but this also makes confronting global problems like the AIDS crisis in Africa unavoidable.

- Instantaneous information flow through global networks yields enormous opportunity but makes irresponsible actions and mistakes globally visible, with massively negative consequences.

When analyzing the above conflicts, it's clear that you can't win by addressing one side without addressing the other. Global supply networks bring corporate risk management, compliance, and governance front and center to make sure the consequences of global actions are visible at the highest levels. Only then can a company respond at a moment's notice.

Supply chains save the world

Think about the implications:

- **Responding to natural disasters**—Only the most resilient supply chains will maintain business continuity during these times of crisis. They will thus be best positioned, as in the Katrina example, to respond to the needs of those affected.
- **Warfare**—In *The World Is Flat: A Brief History of the Twenty-first Century*, Thomas L. Friedman persuasively argues that because of the globalization of the supply chain, there are new interdependencies between nations that make it economically infeasible for them to go to war with one another. They simply can't afford it, creating an economic rather than a military form of mutually-assured destruction.
- **Terrorism**—Again, as more of the world industrializes and a more global middle class is created, the number of potential recruits for terrorist organizations will shrink dramatically.
- **The energy crisis**—We already know that we do not have the resources to support the growing energy needs of an industrializing planet. It won't be government regulation but winning businesses that will solve this problem through innovation. We already see this starting in major corporate initiatives like General Electric's ecomagination or Toyota's success with its hybrid vehicles.
- **World hunger and healthcare**—Who can affordably serve the needs of the Third World other than these companies that have the economic interest and supply chain prowess to make the necessary investments?

If better use and management of the global value chain is what distinguishes winners from losers in product innovation, achieving perfect orders as a supplier, or meeting consumer demand with goods on the shelf, then mastering these capabilities will also lead business, for business reasons, to contribute to solving some of the world's more pressing problems.

We at AMR Research are committed to helping you achieve this goal by continuing to provide research and advice that matters.

Tony Friscia
President and CEO
AMR Research

Supply Chain
Saves the World

Strategy and Policy | 1

Strategy and Policy

Supply chains can save the world, but only with a new model of operation, which AMR Research calls the demand-driven supply network. The power of this model is grounded in business. It provides agility so that cash invested in operations yields quick returns, but without sacrificing liquidity.

Traditional planning cycles are obsolete. Internet connectivity and global markets have accelerated change so dramatically that businesses must revisit daily investments in product development, manufacturing capacity, and inventory. The 21st-century supply chain is no longer about matching supply with demand, but capability with opportunity.

This model may be evolving to serve business, but its mechanics are also the perfect foundation for addressing the world's toughest problems. Faster innovation, more responsive supply networks, and a deeper understanding of customer needs will improve people's lives around the world. New markets mean new consumer benefits.

In Chapter 1, we look at how this model differs from its industrial-era predecessor, how much better it performs operationally, and how businesses are organized around it in three domains: demand, supply, and product. We also identify which companies—our Supply Chain Top 25—best exemplify the model in practice. Finally, we link supply chain leadership to both corporate financial performance and contribution to saving the world.

Demand-Driven Supply Networks: The 21st-Century Supply Chain

*If the customer is king, how well is your business aligned
to serve its sovereign better than anyone else? Supply chain
strategies built in the 20th century were not designed to serve
the customer and, as a result, leave billions of dollars wasted
in idle inventory, redundant work, and errors. The fix is not
just fine-tuning the existing chain, but rebuilding it as a
demand-driven supply network (DDSN).*

Demand-driven supply networks are replacing the factory-
based push supply chains of the 20th century as top companies
learn how customer-centered businesses operate differently.

While "demand-driven supply network" may seem like just
another term for supply chain management, don't be fooled. The
approach attacks areas of business overlooked by traditional supply chain management and promises huge new efficiencies and
growth. Proclaiming that the customer is king is not enough.
Rebuilding the old push supply chain is essential to compete for
profitable growth in the 21st-century business world.

5

DDSN defined

Understanding not only how the demand-driven supply network operates differently but how you can design and build one yourself starts with its definition: a system of technologies and processes that senses and reacts to real-time demand across a network of customers, suppliers, and employees.

Three elements are key to this definition:

- **System**—To be effective, the next-generation supply chain must be scalable. Comprising technology like software applications and databases with business processes, a demand-driven supply network needs a system architecture to scale without compromising flexibility.

- **Demand**—Is demand an order, a forecast, or an opportunity? For demand-driven supply networks to take root, companies must learn to see demand at many levels, complete with buyer willingness to trade off one benefit, say availability, for another, like price. Sensing and reacting to real-time demand does not simply mean to fill the order. It means applying business judgment quickly across all demand.

- **Network**—Contract manufacturers, outsourced design and development, and third-party logistics providers are all part of the rapid transformation of the supply chain away from vertically integrated corporations and toward core-competence-based networks of businesses. For a network to succeed, standards and communication must be pervasive and reliable. The Internet has kicked off this transformation, but its effects have only started to be felt.

Demand-driven strategies start at the "moment of truth"—when supply meets demand. It then works backward to instantiate the supply network that best meets demand. The moment of truth may be a consumer at the supermarket shelf making a choice, a replacement part for a commercial jet waiting for clearance to fly, or full-volume production readiness for this year's hot toy for Christmas. The company best exemplifying this mentality may be Procter & Gamble (P&G), whose Consumer-Driven Supply Network embodies much of what is best in the DDSN model.

Unlike the left-to-right linear chain based on hard assets, the demand-driven supply network looks more like a self-renewing interaction between three strategic business domains: demand, supply, and product (see Figure 1).

What's different?

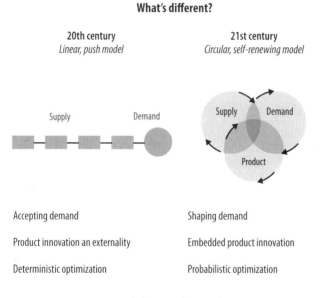

20th century	21st century
Linear, push model	*Circular, self-renewing model*

Accepting demand	Shaping demand
Product innovation an externality	Embedded product innovation
Deterministic optimization	Probabilistic optimization

Figure 1: Demand-driven supply network is the 21st-century supply chain

Visibility and freedom to act in all three domains at once defines the demand-driven business of the 21st century. Before getting there, however, companies must first look at where they've been.

20th-century supply chains are based on the factory, not the consumer

The last century was all about the factory. Marvelous advances were possible through the application of mass production techniques. Henry Ford's fabled River Rouge auto plant was a legend of productive efficiency: rubber, glass, and iron in one end, and cars out the other.

This 20th-century, factory-centric approach accepted demand as a given and pushed identical product through to consumers; as Ford supposedly quipped, "any color you want as long as it's black." Today's supply chain still largely operates as Ford's did, mostly serving the factory, not the consumer. This severely limits the responsiveness of the chain, as recent key metrics of supply chain performance indicate:

· Median time to market for a new product in consumer packaged goods: 27.5 months
· Median days of supply on hand for semiconductor equipment manufacturers: 190 days
· Median order error rate for industrial electronic equipment suppliers: 26 percent

This old approach creates critical deficiencies:

· **The bullwhip effect**—Disruptions downstream ripple back ever louder, creating tremendous demand uncertainty. *Result:* At least $3 trillion in inventory locked in the U.S. and European supply chain as of February 2006.
· **Linear optimization techniques**—Failing to account for variability is fine in a factory with known task cycle times, but it is no good across a network of flexible productive nodes. *Result:* 20 percent order error rate across U.S. industries.

- **No support for product innovation**—The black-box approach to R&D assumes that new products go through the same chain as existing ones. This is slow, wasteful, and error prone. *Result:* 75 percent new product failure rate globally.

One large food and beverage company exemplifies what is wrong. When asked about measurement, this company's supply chain process owner described a rich set of manufacturing utilization and throughput metrics, but with little or nothing tied to commercialization. What suffers is not just efficiency, but growth. New products are hard to launch, promotions are impossible to coordinate, and margins shrink in a deflationary spiral.

DDSN pioneers beat supply chain laggards at the bottom line

AMR Research benchmarking data proves that laggards have an overall cost disadvantage of 5 percent of revenue primarily because of poor forecast accuracy. Such businesses are still serving the factory first and consumers second. They are consequently losing market share and burning up cash with underperforming assets.

Meanwhile, leaders' return on assets (ROA), earnings per share, and profit margin all correlate with the ultimate measure of customer satisfaction: the perfect order (see Figure 2). In addition to cost advantages, these businesses can capitalize upon superior responsiveness to market opportunity to grow and, in many cases, acquire or destroy the laggards. The time to change traditional supply chain practices is now.

9

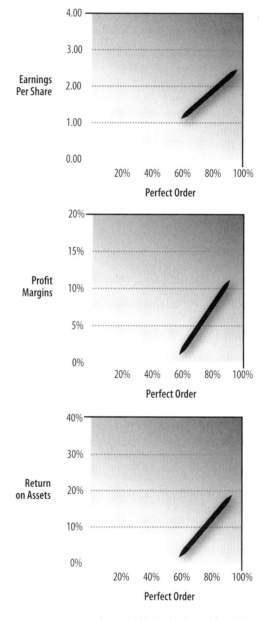

Figure 2: DDSN leadership and financial performance

The next-generation, 21st-century supply network is all about the consumer

This century is all about the consumer. Dell is everyone's favorite example of modern supply chain best practices because it has built a $56 billion business that is fundamentally make to order—the exact opposite of the 1920s-era Ford Motor Company.

Demand drives Dell's network of two dozen key suppliers that accounts for 75 to 80 percent of total spending and provides 80 percent of the R&D effort that gets new products to market. Dell ships 20 million products per quarter with only three days of inventory. Inventory in this model is a liability, not an asset (component prices typically decline 0.5 to 1.0 percent per week).

The business is based on three master performance metrics: growth, profitability, and liquidity. While the first two measure consumer value, the third measures Dell's supply chain agility. This may be the perfect business dashboard for the 21st century.

Dell is the world's best-known example of a demand-driven supply network. What makes Dell great?

It's not just about order to cash. Processes like order to cash or procure to pay are red herrings in demand-driven design. Although they are operational requirements, they provide no strategic direction. Rather, they are essential systems of technologies and processes to deploy and change as needed.

Organization must come first. In nearly 20 years of working with companies on supply chain strategies, AMR Research has learned that processes, while critical, are subservient to organizational design. The factors that determine where a business will compete and how it will gain share and grow profits are really more domains than processes. They naturally tie to three traditional poles of organizational power (other than the CFO): sales, manufacturing, and engineering.

The three strategic DDSN business domains are thus demand management, supply management, and product management.

11

Demand management

Traditional supply chain has largely overlooked demand management, which is defined as the processes required to shape, sense, and respond to demand. These processes include functions in marketing, sales, service, price management, and demand forecasting and planning. Half of the supply-demand balancing problem is demand management.

In a demand-driven supply network, these groups collaborate to manage demand. The sales organization's forecast is a trusted input to operations, and capacity constraints are transparent. Marketing collaborates with supply chain for promotions and new launches. Sales and service rely on logistics for order status. All these inputs come together to create the most accurate view of demand on an ongoing basis.

Ongoing demand visibility is also what radio frequency identification (RFID) is all about. Demand pulsing in rather than being batched periodically gives companies a chance to price higher when the customer is willing to pay. Economists talk about pricing along the demand curve as a way to maximize profits—something the airlines pioneered. Price management fed with unit-level demand data allows for supply-demand balancing with discounts, tiered pricing, and options pricing that do not rely exclusively on physical fulfillment.

Supply management

Common supply management functions include most traditional supply chain functions and roles:

· Direct materials sourcing
· Production operations
· Manufacturing and assembly
· Contract management
· Indirect procurement
· Warehousing and distribution
· Inventory management

Within a DDSN framework, supply management has two levels of activity:

- **Strategic supply management** is the ongoing establishment of supply policies and actual supplier relationships, internal and external, based on a demand-driven supply plan, including integration of network design, logistics planning, capacity planning, stage-gate product development, and sales and operations planning (S&OP).

- **Tactical supply management** links the supply plan to tactical replenishment planning, such as optimal positioning of raw material inventory and supplier capacity, as well as the actual replenishment process itself, including reorder links like electronic data interchange (EDI), vendor-managed inventory, standing supply contracts, and transfer-pricing agreements.

Production operations may reach deeply into shop-floor controls if manufacturing is important to competitive distinction. For businesses with a core competence that is manufacturing based, these controls will increasingly mean the highly flexible automation of production equipment and sensors. Supply management is the domain of robotics.

Otherwise, manufacturing is merely a node of supply in the network, with sourcing rules and processes applied even-handedly across internal and external suppliers. The term "supply network operations" captures this concept of the synchronized execution of manufacturing and logistics processes across a dynamically reconfigurable supply network. Outsourcing decisions, from manufacturing in China to relying on third-party logistics specialists, boil down to whether internal abilities are better and cheaper than what external suppliers can offer.

Best practice means lean flow manufacturing in plants, cross-docking, kitting, customized late-stage assembly in distribution centers, and optimized parts and labor provisioning in field service.

Product management

New product innovation is the main source of new profits and growth, especially as product lifecycles shorten and global markets accelerate the commoditization of existing products. Until recently, most new product development activity was isolated as a cost center in R&D or engineering, and largely overlooked as part of the supply chain.

Demand-driven businesses are those that proactively manage their product lifecycles to introduce new models or product platforms with minimal cannibalization of existing sales. They are also those that assure availability of complementary products essential to acceptance: for example, sufficient game titles to go along with the newest Sony PlayStation.

Far from hoping that R&D will come up with the next great product, the demand-driven supply network requires that product portfolios control customer loyalty, reuse proven technologies, materials, and suppliers, and lock out competition. Including engineering, R&D, and product development functions, this demands explicit collaboration on direct materials sourcing and new product promotions to launch all within stage-gate development processes.

So how do companies get there?

The DDSN roadmap

Building a demand-driven supply network is a transformational journey for most, so a roadmap is essential. Field research on companies making the journey suggests that leap-frogging to highest performance is not realistic, but investments made along the way should be accretive to total business benefit. You have to walk the whole path, but each step has value.

Stages of maturity

AMR Research has developed a DDSN capability model that defines the maturity of an organization's supply network in terms of process (the widespread, advanced, and structured workflows supporting DDSN transformation) and information (timely availability of supply and demand information to support process execution).

The four stages of demand-driven maturity describe how well the network executes to deliver at the moment of truth (see Figure 3):

- **Stage 1: Reacting**—Classic site-to-site traditional supply chain. Integration barely happens.
- **Stage 2: Anticipating**—A connected enterprise. Internal integration, but clumsy external links.
- **Stage 3: Collaborating**—A connected network. External integration, but still no strategic control.
- **Stage 4: Orchestrating**—DDSN plug-and-play external integration. Companies have the ability to create new businesses as opportunity arises.

As organizations progress through these four stages of development, they can institutionalize certain practices. Best practices, like design for supply, lean manufacturing, and S&OP support, are supported by migration up the maturity scale.

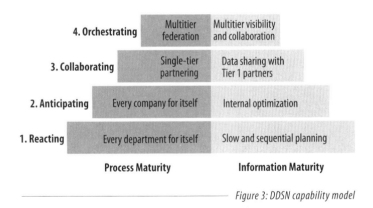

Figure 3: DDSN capability model

	Reacting	Anticipating	Collaborating	Orchestrating
Poster child	Ford c. 1925	Most big ERP users c. 2003	Procter & Gamble c. 2008	??? c. 2010
Goal	Remove variability and waste within functions	Connect functions to create internal process flows	Connect partners to create network process flows	Dynamically reconfigure the supply network
Method	Time and motion studies, work automation	Business process reengineering	Collaborative supply chain	Demand-driven supply network
Margin gain (basis points)	100 to 200	100 to 300	350 to 500	650 to 1,150

Table 1: A history of demand-driven supply networks

Who should lead?

Supply
The most common executive sponsor of AMR Research's clients is the vice president of supply chain. This role is best suited to own accountability for such major business metrics as cost of goods sold, perfect order fulfillment rate, and inventory turns. To function well, it should include purchasing, manufacturing, and logistics. If supply network operations, as defined earlier, makes sense, then an executive with this label would be ideal.

Product
In more than six years of product lifecycle management (PLM) research, we have seen many different potential leaders for the product domain: engineering, R&D, product development, marketing, and even supply chain itself. Product domain leadership is so fundamental to DDSN development that general management may need to create a role accountable for time to market, new product contribution, and perfect product launch. Some companies have created chief innovation officers that might serve this role.

Demand
The obvious starting point is head of sales. Also critical to managing demand, however, are marketing and service. Appropriate business metrics to assign to this include market share, total revenue growth, and gross margin.

What about the CIO?
The CIO has overall accountability for the technical infrastructure that supports demand-driven strategies. This means enforcing standards, identifying critical enablers, and monitoring the timing and sequence of their availability. It also means charting a path that leaves existing systems in place wherever possible and managing all new investment by reallocating existing IT spending.

Making DDSN happen

Identify the leaders for demand, supply, and product domains who are able to lead demand-driven strategies; also plan for those who will resist. Benchmark current performance on metrics of DDSN excellence—forecast accuracy, perfect order performance, time to market—and hone improvement projects with measurable goals against these benchmarks. Finally, look over your shoulder (or ahead) to competitors that are good at responding to demand to see where you are losing business, money, or time.

Understanding the basics of the demand-driven supply network is key to understanding who is winning the supply chain race as determined by the AMR Research Supply Chain Top 25.

STRATEGY AND POLICY

The AMR Research Supply Chain Top 25

PART
TWO

*In November 2004, AMR Research launched the Supply Chain
Top 25, in which we ranked the manufacturers and retailers
that are pioneering the rollout of a new model of supply chain
for the 21st century: the demand-driven supply network.*

The Top 25 identifies the companies that exhibit superior supply chain capability and performance. With superior supply chains
come superior businesses.

Leaders like Dell, P&G, IBM, and Nokia exemplify what the
DDSN model defines as success. All are excellent operationally
while also being brilliant innovators. They are also relentlessly
driven by customers and markets to search for new scalable business opportunity.

In the 2005 edition of the AMR Research Supply Chain Top 25,
we used 2004 information to update the rankings. (Our next Supply Chain Top 25 will be released in November 2006.) Customers
and market demands pushed 2005's leaders to ramp up global supply networks in response to opportunity.

DDSN is now the dominant model for supply chain

Turn back the clock to the days before instantaneous global communication. For most of the 20th century, big factories pumping out identical widgets at low prices was the path to industry dominance. No more. Consumer tastes change too fast, and ideas proliferate quicker than anyone could have imagined 20 years ago, let alone 50 years ago when the rules for industry were formed (namely capital markets, labor relations, and government regulation).

How will the 20th-century supply chain satisfy consumers? It can't. Consumer demand is killing off companies and industries left and right. Only those that master demand-driven strategies will survive.

DDSN strategy and the predator's supply chain

Mastery of the DDSN model may still be years away for even the best of today's leaders, but the model has clearly taken root. Last year's Top 25 outperformed their peers in terms of ROA, days sales outstanding, and innovation. They also saw a 2.9 percent average share price bump, simply because they were recognized as having a Top 25 supply chain, according to a Lehigh University study entitled "Does Supply Chain Excellence Pay?—New Evidence" (by Nandkumar Nayar, the Hans J. Bär Chair and Professor of Finance at Lehigh's College of Business and Economics). These may be statistical anomalies or self-fulfilling prophecies, but our benchmarks show these companies as having better margins, ROA, and earnings per share.

Consider the following:

· P&G (No. 2) acquired Gillette in 2005.
· Wal-Mart's (No. 8) U.S. market share grew to 17.1 percent in 2004 from 6.8 percent in 1992.
· Dell's (No. 1) PC market share has grown 16.2 percent to 18.9 percent since 1995.
· Nike's (No. 21) shoe sales grew at a 10.1 percent compound annual growth rate (CAGR) between 1995 and 2005.

Demand-driven strategies give these companies a predator's edge.

	Company	Comments
1	Dell	Still the defining DDSN business, Dell maintained excellent financial and operational performance while growing the top line almost 20%.
2	Procter & Gamble	P&G climbed to No. 2 with its Consumer-Driven Supply Network strategy, supporting growth both organically and through acquisition.
3	IBM	On demand may have limits as a marketing strategy, but it is representative of how this tech giant manages its global supply network—lean, profitable, and innovative, all the way from chips to consultants.
4	Nokia	Nokia dropped two notches from 2004 with lower growth in 2004, but it still led in both operational excellence and innovation.
5	Toyota	Toyota's ability to capitalize on hot demand for hybrids is exactly what a demand-driven supply network should deliver.
6	Johnson & Johnson	Supply chain complexity, from medical devices to basic supermarket items, does not keep J&J from delivering growth, more profitability, and better-than-peer-group inventory turns.
7	Samsung Electronics	New to the Top 25, Samsung rode a strong year in electronics to huge growth and profitability.
8	Wal-Mart	Wal-Mart ranks No. 4 in AMR Research's Opinion of DDSN leadership. It weathered a challenging year with little dropoff in operational performance.
9	Tesco	Even with lower growth, UK-based Tesco outperformed its peers dramatically in operations and profitability.
10	Johnson Controls	JCI continued to innovate aggressively on its engineering and operational links with the hypercomplex automotive supply chain. It may be the world's best supplier business.

Table 2: The AMR Research Supply Chain Top 25 for 2005

	Company	Comments
11	Intel	Intel is the rare player that orchestrates supply networks from the back end forward. By managing and shaping demand all the way to consumers, this DDSN leader softens the blow of hugely inflexible production assets.
12	Anheuser-Busch	With extraordinary visibility to consumer demand at the point of sale and best-in-class distribution, A-B is able to create demand as well as meet it.
13	Woolworths	Woolworths continues to pioneer DDSN principles. It has the growth, profitability, and operational performance to show for it.
14	The Home Depot	Home Depot's visibility skyrocketed as disaster response in the U.S. Southeast showcased its flexibility and scale. Solid numbers across the board prove that social responsibility is more than just good community relations.
15	Motorola	The turnaround of Motorola, another new company to the Top 25, demonstrates demand-driven principles all the way from design for supply chain through reverse logistics. A cool product (the RAZR) doesn't hurt either.
16	PepsiCo	Diversified and nimble, PepsiCo's brands deliver growth with innovation and minimal sacrifices in operational performance.
17	Best Buy	Best Buy's excellent basic operations are a foundation for growth that may include a big push into private label merchandise— leveraging the brand with supply chain.
18	Cisco Systems	Cisco's Internet-era power is returning, with results that reflect a classic demand-driven strategy: heavy and early reliance on a global supply network, but wise to the ways of demand visibility.
19	Texas Instruments	TI invested many years ago in advanced planning systems. With a surging electronics sector in 2004, these systems came in handy.

	Company	Comments
20	Lowe's	Outgrowing archrival Home Depot, Lowe's excels at store operations and the consumer experience. Lagging in ROA and inventory turns may be a fair tradeoff for gains in market share.
21	Nike	Nike's global supply network has earned it PR static in the past, but better-than-peer ROA and inventory turns show plenty of operational skill, while 12% growth is just reward for best-in-class product (and brand) innovation.
22	L'Oreal	20% ROA is the highest among our Top 25. By shaping demand around great brands, L'Oreal makes money for investors.
23	Publix Super Markets	With an ROA eight times higher than peer average and 10% growth, Publix enters the Top 25 and looks to have a promising future.
24	Sysco	The "other" Sysco, this food service giant has pioneered some of the demand-driven practices most likely to matter as feeding the world gains attention.
25	Coca-Cola	While down from 2004's No. 17 rank, Coca-Cola continues to lead the development of cutting-edge demand analytics with its DDSN strategy.

The Supply Chain Top 25 is a combination of what is publicly known about each company's past performance augmented with AMR Research's analysis of future earning potential as dictated by supply chain dominance.

The first component of the ranking is publicly available financial data, which comprises 60 percent of the total score: return on assets and inventory turns each account for 25 percent, and trailing 12 months' growth accounts for 10 percent. The second component of the ranking is AMR Research's opinion, which is 40 percent of the total score. The opinion component is based on a structured voting methodology across AMR Research's team of analysts. These scores lead to a composite score from which the rankings are determined.

The importance of demand-driven supply networks

First, demand-driven supply networks are an organizational structure. Instead of departments extending from R&D, through production, to sales in a linear way, DDSN encompasses three overlapping areas of responsibility:

- **Demand**—Customer service and market creation
- **Supply**—Traditional operations, including sourcing, manufacturing, and distribution
- **Product**—R&D, engineering, design, and all elements of product innovation

The heads of these areas should ideally be executive VP level or above. The structure can also accommodate extensive management of external partners. Conceptually, demand-driven supply networks are more like self-reinforcing cycles than an assembly line handoff. The big differences between the old school and the demand-driven way are in shaping market demands, embedding product innovation in operations, and managing variability mathematically.

Information technology's role

Demand-driven strategies can only work with massive amounts of IT investment. Luckily, most of this investment was made during the Internet bubble. Now is the time to take advantage of it.

DDSN leaders use IT to improve communication, visibility, and decision making across supply, demand, and product domains. Individual IT projects or initiatives should be about connecting work processes to increase speed, quality, and profitability of everything from customer orders to new product launches.

The practicalities of organizing for demand-driven supply networks require massive amounts of information and constant back and forth with customers and partners. Everything from full-featured 3D computer-aided design (CAD) models to EDI orders depends on the IT stack—from the microchip to the user (or machine) interface.

The actual pieces of this structure are usually known by their initials—ERP, SCM, PLM, RDB, and so on. Each is likely to have cost the companies on our list tens or hundreds of millions of dollars.

Yes, there was oversell during the 1990s tech boom, and the perpetual license sales model was bad for customers, but the systems largely work. Demand-driven leaders are getting plenty of return on investment, provided they blend best practices and innovative IT applications, and don't rely exclusively on packaged software.

Honorable mention

A number of companies received high voter totals from our panel of experts. Four of these rank among the Top 25 in pure AMR Research opinion scoring, but they failed to make the list in the overall composite score. This means AMR Research sees extensive progress toward the DDSN model and thus a strong future for these companies, even if their financial results for 2004 held them back in our calculation. Here are the four:

- Nissan, which fell out of the Top 25 because of a dropoff in growth, remains a leader in terms of demand-driven principles and continues to deliver outstanding profits.
- Hewlett-Packard (HP), which also fell out of the Top 25 because of a much lower growth figure after integrating the Compaq acquisition, made big strides in operating performance and is positioned with new leadership to keep gaining ground.
- Target, a pioneer in retailer branding, is bringing fashion to the masses.
- Staples has a supply chain approach that reaches all the way to shelf performance.

The Supply Chain Top 25 in context

AMR Research has been analyzing demand-driven practices for several years. One of the major findings of our research is that supply chain performance, understood in DDSN terms, is characterized by a hierarchy of supply chain metrics, including perfect order rate, total supply chain costs, and demand forecast accuracy (see "Diagnosing Your Supply Chain Health With the Metrics That Matter" in Chapter 6). Combining these metrics with a high-level measurement of product innovation success, like time to value, gives a good picture of both the ongoing profitability of a business and its prospects for future growth.

Our research makes it clear that leadership in demand-driven performance is related directly to a company's overall financial performance. Supply chain leaders are able to shape demand, instantly respond to market changes, and crush their competitors. According to AMR Research benchmarking data, leaders carry 15 percent less inventory, are 60 percent faster to market, and complete 17 percent more perfect orders. These advantages separate predators from prey.

Business and financial leaders have come to recognize the strategic importance of supply chain. These 25 companies are defining the future of supply chain and giving their companies a predator's edge.

DDSN Leaders: Making Profits and Saving the World

*So what does it really mean to make the Supply Chain Top 25?
How about higher share value? The demand-driven supply
network is about much more than efficiency. It's a new way of
doing business, one that directly affects the bottom line.*

When we published the first Supply Chain Top 25 in 2004, most
of the companies named reacted favorably, as befits the compli-
ment. A handful recognized the potential message this sends to
investors about which companies' abilities justify higher investor
expectations and thus higher share price/earnings multiples.

But some stayed stuck in a supply chain efficiency mindset, focusing exclusively on the movement of materials.

Operational efficiency is only half the story

What separates those who really understand demand-driven concepts from those who don't is that success in the 21st century depends on embedding product innovation in supply chain management.

A heated conversation with the lead supply chain executive at one company listed in the 2004 Top 25 made this gap in understanding clear. This executive saw the list and concluded the criteria must be ridiculous because, in a recent analysis of his own operation, the company was a mess. How could it possibly be listed as a leader when it had rested on the laurels of its product innovation while maintaining a sloppy manufacturing and logistics operation?

The answer is that DDSN leaders do more than sell the same old junk for a few dollars less. Being demand driven means embracing customer demand completely enough to bring a steady stream of valuable new products and services to market as well as maintain excellent operations. Companies that consistently do both are more than just rare—they are a new breed. Looking out 10 years, this breed will force all others to the margins of business.

The executive in question was missing this point: his operational effectiveness might be subpar, but his company's innovation was strong enough to prop up the metrics that matter, like ROA and inventory turns. Imagine how valuable this company will be once operations are keeping pace with innovation. AMR Research benchmarking research indicates that the incremental operating margins available to demand-driven leaders that get this will be between 450 and 1,220 basis points higher than their peers.

Efficiency plus innovation equals better cash flow

Of the top 25 nonfinancial companies in the S&P 100 in order of total free cash flow generated in 2003, 10 were on our 2004 Top 25. And in 2004 and 2005, the companies on our list topped the S&P 500 and Dow Jones average. These are not coincidences: DDSN leadership means higher profitability. Clearly, financial executives are looking for insight into how this works.

28

Excellence is not just a lot of "Eureka!" moments

It boils down to reducing the time between budgeting a new idea and earning back all development expenses (time to value). Systematically attacking this time-to-value issue while pursuing demand-driven strategies requires at least three changes:

- Adhere to a formal new product development and launch process.
- Establish design-for-X programs, where X may be postponement, manufacturability, service, or any of a number of supply-chain-based business goals.
- Manage all product innovation decisions with portfolio management principles rather than simply as a series of projects.

Operational excellence is a well-established and worthy goal. But without constantly renewing products offered to customers, there will be little value in such excellence. Ask yourself: how valuable is the world's most efficient typewriter manufacturer today?

DDSN value	Fixed capital managers	Tier n manufacturers	Original equipment manufacturers (OEMs)
	Bulk chemicals	Components	Consumer electronics
	Metals	Assemblies	Consumer packaged goods
	Pulp and paper	Textiles	
	Agriculture	Packaging	Aerospace (primes)
	Semiconductors	Ingredients	Pharmaceuticals
			Apparel
			Automotive
Operating margin advantage	250–760 basis points	300–790 basis points	450–1,220 basis points
Macro profit potential (United States)	$30B to $93B per year	$36B to $97B per year	$111B to $299B per year
DDSN macro profit total = $177B to $488B			

Table 3: Estimates of DDSN incremental operating margin effects

29

More at stake than just money

Since AMR Research began covering the Supply Chain Top 25, we have been peppered with questions about the methodology and implications of the underlying research on demand-driven supply networks. One observation through all of this is that supply chain and operations professionals are ambitious, driven, and eager to be measured as they work to enhance the competitiveness of their companies.

Many professionals in the supply chain world are beginning to see that this is a game for all the marbles. High-profile acquisitions often involve a dominant supply chain consuming a weaker one. Locations are closed, people relocated, and jobs eliminated.

For the best companies—and, perhaps even more importantly, the best individuals—fear motivates less than aspiration in making a difference. When Katrina struck the Gulf Coast and companies like P&G, Wal-Mart, and Home Depot marshaled their supply chains to help, we saw what demand-driven excellence offers society at large.

Feeding the hungry, discovering and delivering medicines, and greening our economy may be encouraged by the United Nations or Greenpeace, but it will be accomplished in the private sector. Sustainable delivery of fuel-efficient hybrid cars or refrigerated trucks full of food will ultimately come not from government agencies or charitable donations, but from companies like those in the Supply Chain Top 25.

Doing well by doing good

Business is not about saving the world. True corporate leaders, however, see that long-term growth depends on finding new markets by matching not just supply to demand, but capability to opportunity. Whether the opportunity is a 100 mile per gallon vehicle or a $20 cell phone targeting two billion third-world consumers, the capability falls squarely on the shoulders of the 21st-century supply chain. It's starting to look like the companies that can save the world might also be the ones making all the money.

Supply Chain Globalization | 2

Supply Chain Globalization

Cast as a villain by some and savior by others, globalization represents huge opportunity, but also grave threat. Survey data collected among several hundred U.S. manufacturing executives in 2003 and 2004, for instance, shows a sudden lurch away from viewing China as a source of cheap supply to a potential competitor. The issue is central to business success.

Beyond globalization's meaning to business, there are effects on the environment, social justice, and human health. Many worry that developing nations joining the consumer society will devastate global ecology. Some also fear the spread of disease and potentially harmful technology. Yet hope springs eternal that huge numbers of people may soon have access to better consumer goods, jobs, and education. The common thread in these debates is supply chain, whether this means selling to or sourcing from the global market.

In Chapter 2, we explore how supply chain globalization affects business strategy, first by looking at new opportunities for growth in both the developed and developing worlds. We offer lessons on how companies organize to cope with global markets and highlight research on how product innovation is engaging partners worldwide. Finally, we provide field research on the unique risks in doing business in China.

Sustainable Growth Is Not About Lower Costs

Growth is the one goal that all businesses pursue. Shareholder value is created when a business can project sustainable growth into its profit stream. Through the last century, this meant getting a scale position in an industry like automotive, plastics, or packaged foods, and selling more units of the same basic products while cutting costs.

With this formula, big business managed its major markets, North America and Europe, as demand centers, while its secondary markets, Asia (until the 1980s) and the so-called "Rest of World," were primarily seen as suppliers of raw material or cheap labor. This formula doesn't work anymore.

We are entering a new age. The arrival of the Internet turned Rest of World into an opportunity, not just for low-cost labor, but for new customers, new ideas, and entirely new businesses. This idea has been popularized in books like Thomas L. Friedman's *The World Is Flat* and *The Fortune at the Bottom of the Pyramid: Eradicating Poverty Through Profits* by C.K. Prahalad.

Beneath the surface, this idea depends on a global supply network that operates in real time, with high visibility, and in fundamentally more innovative ways than ever imagined possible by the industrial engineers who created Ford's River Rouge mega-factory.

IT matters, but not without a new model of supply chain: DDSN

The inflection point is widely misunderstood as a revolution in information technology. IT has certainly been a big growth engine and vital to the tremendous productivity growth rates of three to five percent a year since 1995 (versus one to two percent for most of the 20th century). But IT, which has been around for 50 years, has only recently contributed to serious productivity gains. Why? IT applied to traditional linear push supply chains brought only minimal gains to business. Remember the famous quip, "We see IT everywhere but in the productivity statistics"?

The real breakthrough has been the development of demand-driven supply networks (DDSNs). They use IT far more intensively than linear push supply chains, for which computerization basically allows materials to be tracked through production. Decision makers in demand-driven companies use IT to weigh choices across all three major domains of a business: supply management, demand management, and product management.

The operating difference between push supply chains with computers attached and information-rich, demand-driven supply networks is dramatically superior flexibility in manufacturing and distribution. The data proving this includes time to market for new products that has been slashed 50 to 70 percent across industries, inventory-to-sales ratios that are less than half of what they were two decades ago, and the number of unique products available that is 10 times higher today than in 1980. This means that growth opportunities that would have been subscale and thus unattractive investments in 1975 often make the cut today.

The next frontier—sustainable growth in a global economy

Looking ahead for growth made viable with the DDSN model, two realms of opportunity emerge. One is finding innovative and sustainable products and services for developed-world consumers, which generally have all the hamburgers, t-shirts, and televisions they need. The first world has become an economy of abundance. Its citizens do not need more stuff, but *better* stuff: fuel-efficient vehicles, safe and affordable medical services, security for families...the list is almost endless. Demand-driven supply networks can make these growth markets commercially viable and, in the process, improve the quality of life.

Consider the following growth opportunities:

· Healthcare expenditure per capita in real terms has grown faster than GDP in the Organization for Economic Co-operation and Development (OECD) countries for 9 of the last 10 years. On average, the rate has been about 60 percent higher.

· Hybrid vehicle unit sales in the United States have seen an 85 percent compound annual growth rate (CAGR) since 2000. Similar growth has occurred in shipments of photovoltaic units for solar energy production.

· Information product sales, as tracked by the U.S. Commerce Department, are 87 times greater than they were in 1947, while manufactured product sales are 23 times greater and agricultural product sales are only 7 times greater.

The traditional major markets in North America and Europe look more likely to deliver growth in biotech and healthcare, clean and sustainable consumer durables, and pure content products, like iPod downloads, than in cheaper widgets.

Rest of World: the fastest-growing market

The other big opportunity is in those markets traditionally dismissed in business planning as Rest of World. The developing world is still an economy of scarcity. Businesses seeking growth will get more by building a consumer supply chain to serve this economy than by scraping out truckloads of cheap raw materials for an already over-served first world.

Demand-driven supply networks do two things differently here. First, they sense and react to demand with products packaged and priced to suit low-income shoppers; C.K. Prahalad details this story in *The Fortune at the Bottom of the Pyramid*. Global companies like P&G and Unilever have substantial and growing initiatives in these countries because growth in stable-population countries, like the United States, Japan, and Germany, is so tough.

"In last year's sustainability report, I identified three key challenges that P&G faces as we work toward this vision:

1. *To create new businesses with sufficient scale to fund research and develop-ment and market development costs*

2. *To develop new business models appropriate to lower income, developing-country markets*

3. *To lower costs to make products affordable in undeveloped markets that lack large-scale supply chain and distribution efficiencies that are normal in richer, developed markets*

"P&G's safe drinking water work is a good example of the progress we're mak-ing in all three areas. We've chosen this as a key focus area based on the United Nations Millennium Development Goal of providing improved access to safe drinking water.

"We are only starting to turn our vision into reality. But imagine a world where corporations, in partnerships with civil society and government, can significantly deliver on the UN Millennium Development Goal of addressing the world's most critical health issues. This improvement in society will provide the foundation for sustainable growth."

—George D. Carpenter, director of Corporate Sustainable Development, P&G

"Unilever's products are sold in 150 different countries. To succeed, we must listen to consumers and tailor our products to suit different markets, tastes, habits, and pockets. Respecting these differences is at the core of our approach.

"Everyone, regardless of income level, likes using high-quality, innovative products on occasions when looking and feeling good are important. We try to make our products accessible in terms of price and affordability, sometimes by offering them in small, affordable sachets. This makes world-class quality products attainable by more consumers. For example, in sub-Saharan Africa, Unilever offers several everyday products in small pack sizes priced at less than 10 cents, such as Royco soups, Close-Up toothpaste, Omo laundry powder, and Sunsilk shampoo.

"In 2004, we compared the price of our lowest-priced food and home and personal care products in 82 countries (covering 90 percent of our global turnover) with that country's daily minimum wage. In 52 countries, our lowest-price food product is less than five percent of the minimum daily wage."

—*Unilever Social Report, 2004*

Sourcing with respect

The second aspect demand-driven supply networks do differently is source across a network of suppliers rather than just chase lower costs. Nike learned the hard way that sweatshop labor is a double-edged sword. Cheap labor is not a sustainable advantage. As the apparel industry is discovering to its dismay, the longer lead times that come with Asian suppliers often wipe out savings with markdowns. Cheap raw materials are also no longer meaningful as global commodity markets level the playing field for manufacturers downstream.

"Phil Knight said it over five years ago: to be successful in business in the 21st century, you must successfully integrate corporate responsibility into the heart of the business. Doing this is a sometimes uncomfortable, frustrating adventure in the unknown. It is made painful when efforts are taken out of context and turned into news headlines. It is made worthwhile every time we see the positive impact our company and our employees have on a young person's life, or on workers in our supply chain. It is reinforced every time we see employees integrating corporate responsibility into their day-to-day work and coming up with innovative, appealing products that push the boundaries in both design and sustainability.

"This is what drives us. We are in it for the long term. As everyone at Nike says so often, there is no finish line."

—*Mark Parker and Charlie Denson, co-presidents, Nike Brand*

A leader's approach is demonstrated by HP, which intensively cultivates its overseas suppliers' knowledge and integration into the supply chain to minimize disruptions and improve efficiency. The trend will not abate as mega-supplier China continues its push upmarket "selling more advanced products with fatter profit margins" (as stated in *The New York Times* article "Rising Yuan Pushes China Upmarket," April 20, 2006). If two heads are better than one, shouldn't six billion be better than one billion?

Consider the following data:

· United Nations Development Programme (UNDP) data shows that exports as a percentage of GDP for developing nations grew to 35 percent from 25 percent between 1990 and 2003, while those for high-income OECD countries grew 4 percentage points to 21 percent.

· UNDP data also shows that manufactured goods as a percentage of total exports grew to 73 percent from 58 percent between 1990 and 2003 for developing nations, while high-income OECD countries barely grew at all, just 1 percentage point to 79 percent of total exports between 1990 and 2003.

- High-tech exports as a percentage of total merchandise exports grew from 0 to 21 percent between 1990 and 2003 for developing nations, while high-income OECD saw this figure remain flat at 18 percent.
- Finally, imports as a percentage of GDP grew in developing nations to 33 percent from 24 percent between 1990 and 2003, while high-income OECD countries saw only a 3 percentage point rise to 21 percent of GDP.

The data says that the developing world is growing faster than the developed world not only in terms of selling into the global supply network, but buying from it. Further, the developing world's growth is fastest among the highest value-added manufacturing sectors. We are not talking sweatshops and banana plantations—the game is about engaging this next frontier with respect to building platforms for sustainable profit growth.

Supply chain saves the world

AMR Research has been studying the role of information technology in manufacturing and supply chain for 20 years. All along the promise of better, faster, and cheaper has sustained our clients in their efforts to build better enterprise resource planning (ERP) systems, factory automation, product development processes, and regulatory compliance controls. These tools are the machinery of the 21st-century supply chain, which is now wrestling with globalization. The opportunity is there. Growth is happening, but change is inevitable. Leaders need to seize the chance now.

Organizing for the Global Enterprise

Industry leaders like P&G, Unilever, General Mills, SABMiller, Nestle, Heineken, Johnson & Johnson, and Novartis have made the structure and governance model of the global organization a top executive concern. They realize that structure needs to follow strategy, but how?

Companies must define a global strategy for innovation and demand-driven operations first. Only then can an effective global organization be designed and put in place.

When it comes to organizing for the global supply chain, structure follows strategy. Get the strategy right, and the structure will become clear. However, no one model fits all. The right structure is dependent on understanding five factors:

· Business vision
· Model of future business structure
· Culture, leadership, and governance
· Business process architecture
· IT applications and information structure

Demand-driven strategies need to define global strategies

Being demand driven requires that the organizational structure support the operating strategy across the full value chain, which stretches from the point of consumption back to operations and fulfillment. Demand-driven supply networks require performance metrics that are interlinked throughout the organization. For example, manufacturing can't cut cost at the expense of customer service levels. Manufacturing and customer-facing groups must work together to make sure the ultimate benefit is a profitable perfect order. When these metrics are not linked and are used out of context, you get the classic dysfunctional organization.

Demand-driven leaders support their operating strategy in the following ways:

· **Create value networks.** Accountabilities and reporting relationships across the network need to be aligned and connected to operational goals. Manufacturing is no longer just accountable for what happens in the plant, or able to concern itself with only capacity and utilization issues. It must also make sure the right product is on the shelf. On the opposite end, R&D must consider manufacturing when designing products, and marketing can't set expectations that manufacturing can't meet.

· **Involve cross-functional teams in joint value creation.** These teams, which include R&D, operations, finance, and sales and marketing, meet in what are often called top-to-top meetings with important customers. Organizations are starting to understand that it's not just about sharing information across their functional boundaries, but actually jointly creating value. As such, product supply becomes about customer service, with the team members from various parts of the organization becoming critical members of account planning.

· **Use S&OP processes to execute global business strategies.** The constitution, structure, and mandate of the global sales and operations planning (S&OP) process support the global business strategy. This is where companies uncover the most profitable demand-shaping activities and determine how to best align supply to capture market opportunities.

- **Recognize the need for improved demand and supply visibility signals.** As organizations become more global, demand and supply visibility become more critical, and customer scorecard performance becomes the measure of success. Only 22 percent of companies, however, are actively using customer scorecards to judge operational performance, recent AMR Research data shows. This must change.
- **Realize the right IT infrastructure makes a difference.** To support shifts in business, the supporting IT infrastructure, tools, and resources need to align with the emerging requirements and structure to help improve visibility and the sensing of demand from downstream data.

From the outside in

For each company, the organizational structure will be determined by business goals, governance structures, and leadership model.

The organizational structure has to be designed from the outside in. This requires looking from the point of consumption back to manufacturing and R&D, and then deciding on the organization needed. Should customer account management and product launch be a global or a local issue? The answer is largely determined by market dynamics and channel priorities.

There's no one recipe for the perfect organization. Companies must look at their own business goals and organize to how they best penetrate the market. For example, in the pharmaceutical industry, most product launches are global and centralized, launching simultaneously in core markets that have different regulatory agencies. But in consumer products, a major global account like Wal-Mart may require a global strategy in which joint value creation is centralized, but execution is decentralized and carried out in local markets. This structure can be more distributed with a strong governance foundation.

The three models from which to choose are decentralized, centralized, or a hybrid. Which one is right is determined by a company's needs. Companies should not rush into reorganizing for a global market until they understand which of the three models fits best:

- **Decentralized**—This is best suited for a company with different products for different markets. Cargill fits this model.
- **Centralized**—A company with a strong centralized leadership, process, and standards model—and typically one with a strong global brand—fits here. Heineken follows this model.
- **Hybrid**—A company with a global growth model that has a mix of regional-specific and global brands uses this model. P&G, Unilever, and SABMiller can be found here.

Location on the demand-driven journey determines structure

The journey to becoming demand driven and building a demand-driven supply network typically follows four stages of progression (as described in Chapter 1):

- Stage 1: Reacting
- Stage 2: Anticipating
- Stage 3: Collaborating
- Stage 4: Orchestrating

In the first three stages, the organization is clearly focused on product supply. Aligned with physical assets, it is heavily weighted toward traditional manufacturing. Transition begins in the third and fourth stages, which are characterized by strong global S&OP and new product launch abilities. It demands top-down executive leadership similar to the kind seen at Dell and P&G.

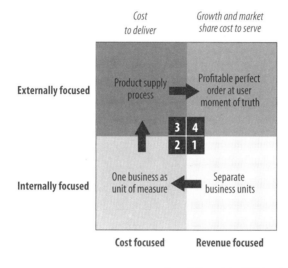

Figure 1: The evolving DDSN transformation

Companies also tend to be more cross-functionally organized across processes, planning globally while executing locally. Most of the top global manufacturing companies can be plotted somewhere between Stages 2 and 3. To back these processes, they are invoking the concept of geographic hubs, using them as intermediate steps on the consolidation journey. Some consumer goods manufacturers have already organized processes around the hubs of North America, Africa, South America, Asia, and so forth. This facilitates regional learning and makes value creation easier. If you have an African hub, everyone is dealing with Africa and understands its market. Imagine the difficulty if Nigeria and England were put in the same hub: half of the organization's effort would go toward trying to understand the local differences. Regional hubs make the differences immaterial, thus eliminating the complexity of trying to converge a global organization, with all its differences, into one.

Smart companies then use the hubs to gradually build a global operation, since creating a global operations and IT organization must be done in steps. At companies like SABMiller and P&G, leaders from the regional hubs meet a few times a year to share best practices and lessons learned. The practices and lessons that resonate can then be turned into global standards and strategies as need be. On a side note for global IT organizations, this is also a pragmatic approach to global master data management, an area with which many IT groups are grappling.

Where to begin?

Before jumping into an organizational redesign, start first with business goals, culture, leadership, market requirements, and governance models. Understand these dimensions before changing anything. A common mistake companies make is to blindly follow another organization's restructuring model without understanding the context.

48

The next step is to identify the gaps in current business performance and missed market opportunities based on the customer experience. Start with the moments of truth of demand-driven supply networks—the customer's purchase, usage experience, service of a long-life product, and final disposal—and move backward. Design the organization and integrated system of processes and metrics based on the delivery of customer excellence in these moments of truth.

Also, don't forget the architecture of IT infrastructure that will support the new global business operating model. Industry leaders focus their attention on master data management, downstream demand visibility, one global organization, a single face to the customer, consolidation to a single instance of an application (such as ERP), and IT benefits realization. These are practical, value-adding, foundational elements that improve organizational agility and help lead the architecture redesign that will support the emerging global organization.

In the final design, ask these questions to check that organizational redesign efforts are moving in the right direction:

- Does the structure support the global leadership model?
- How will the structure affect global business performance and reporting?
- How will products be launched and brands built?
- Does the structure support global cost-cutting priorities?
- How will the structure affect the global management of innovation in the organization?
- How will the structure support developing global customer accounts?
- How will the organization learn globally, and how will it use its scale with the new structure?
- What shared service and outsourcing opportunities exist, and how will they be supported?
- What is the strategy to manage the changing organization?

Taking Innovation Global

Accelerated innovation is the linchpin of long-term corporate growth in manufacturing. When you take it global, however, you also increase the complexity—a necessary evil in keeping shareholders satisfied and meeting the needs of the world.

Global innovation is testing the resource constraints of companies, leading some to tap into an affordable pool of global design expertise to meet the speed to market required.

Why innovate?

The answer is simple: innovative companies do better financially than their peers. The companies on *BusinessWeek*/Boston Consulting Group's list of the top 25 innovators for 2005 had median profit growth of 3.4 percent a year since 1995 versus 0.4 percent for the S&P Global 1200. Global markets increasingly play a stronger role in financial performance, shaping corporate strategies to better meet the needs of a broader customer base. Consider the following:

- General Electric (GE) saw 1Q06 revenue from outside the United States jump 10 percent, with orders increasing 21 percent in China and a whopping 66 percent in Africa and the Middle East.
- QUALCOMM is expanding its engineering by opening new design centers around the world. Complementing its U.S. design operations, the telecom chip manufacturer is adding engineering teams in Germany, India, and the UK to provide complete systems to an expanding customer base and worldwide marketplace.

These companies are finding that collaborating with business partners for new product development and introduction (NPDI) is directly linked to superior operating margin growth. It's a fact backed by a recent IBM survey of 765 CEOs. The survey found that companies with superior operating margin growth received 33 percent more ideas for product, strategy, and process innovations from external partners than those with inferior margin growth. The top benefits of external collaboration cited by the CEOs are reduced costs, improved quality and customer satisfaction, and access to skills and products.

An AMR Research survey of 485 companies on the use of outsourced engineering services turned up similar benefits. According to respondents, the top benefits generated by outsourcing (one form of external collaboration) are reduced costs and improved profit levels, on-time performance and time to market (generated by access to skilled resources), and improved quality (see Figure 2).

Q: What benefits/improvements do you expect to achieve through the outsourcing of NPDI/engineering services?

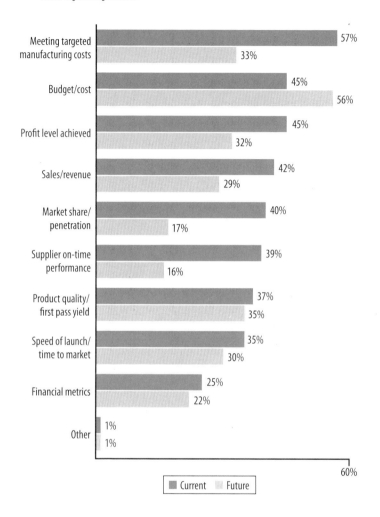

% responses represent organizations evaluating NPDI outsourcing in 2006–2007

Figure 2: Current and future benefits from NPDI outsourcing

Combining the results from the two surveys reveals that companies using outsourced engineering services are increasing their ability to deliver innovation and improving company financial performance.

Manufacturers are taking heed, with the numbers increasing of those looking outside their own companies to find the talent and resources to meet today's global demands. The aforementioned AMR Research survey found 30 percent are outsourcing some portion of the NPDI process. While 40 percent expect to evaluate outsourcing within the next two years, it remains a complementary approach to internal product design, with most companies outsourcing no more than 15 percent of their design engineering activities.

The need for speed

Accelerating product to market is the main factor behind outsourcing innovation. Consider the following:

· Nearly half of survey respondents cite slow time to market as the top problem they are trying to fix.
· Penetrating new markets with existing products and enhancements is expected to be behind future outsourcing.
· Using investments in existing products remains a priority, with 43 percent seeking to add new features and lower production or operational costs.

Q: For what types of products and problems will you consider outsourcing engineering services?

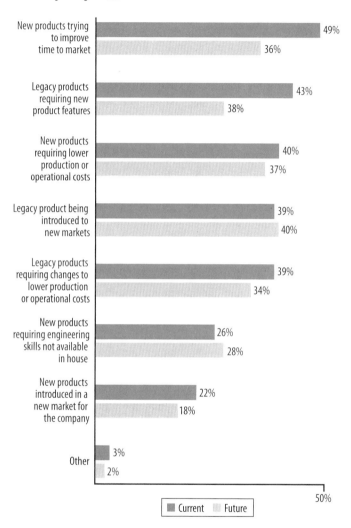

% responses represent organizations evaluating NPDI outsourcing in 2006–2007

Figure 3: Problems addressed with NPDI outsourcing

It's not just noncore activities that are being outsourced. Despite the fact that 73 percent of the companies consider engineering design a core competency, 30 percent currently outsource a part of their NPDI process, and another 40 percent are planning on outsourcing within the next two years.

Companies are looking beyond the traditional core versus noncore decision for outsourcing, considering outsourced engineering services as a way to provide competitive advantage. They are betting top-line growth on the success of outsourcing.

Outsourcing pieces of new product activities is becoming an essential part of a company's strategy. However, success is not guaranteed. Companies report that they must provide additional management and have strong governance in order to maximize the benefits of outsourcing.

Product success takes on many characteristics as customer appetite for greater choice increases. This demand is forcing manufacturers to respond faster with new products that are increasing in complexity. Delivering product complexity faster into a global market has forced manufacturers to assess new approaches to finding the resources necessary for success.

Facing the Fifth Dragon: Succeeding in China

Japan, Hong Kong, Singapore, and South Korea gained global economic prominence following World War II as the "dragon economies." Now a fifth dragon joins the list: China. Those heading there to take advantage of the country's bustling economy need to plan on at least five years before payback, say those who have already gone.

Although only 676 miles separate Shanghai from Beijing, the two cities are worlds apart. Shanghai, at the center of commerce, is the fire of the fifth-dragon economy, fueling growth. Beijing, the center of government, is making policy as the head of the dragon. Tension between these two forces is affecting the development of a supply chain management strategy for China, with the rule of law, social responsibility, and protection of intellectual property (IP) at the center of the debate. These will be issues for the next 10 years.

The conspicuous absence of the rule of law

China has no clear separation of government and commerce. While the state has relaxed control of state-owned enterprises and the economy has opened, the role of the government official is still confused. In the words of Pat Powers, director of China operations at the US-China Business Council, "We have to make friends with Chinese administrators, we have to court them, and we have to help them to help you. While they should just process paperwork, they don't."

HP's director of supply chain for China, Chin Chye Lim, echoed similar thoughts: "It is not what you know, but who you know that makes a difference in China. My advice is to work closely with government officials."

Throw away conventional understanding of what a government agency should do. Instead, expect government administrators to set their own rules, and expect that advice to be circular, contradictory, and confusing. Relationships will guide the efforts, not a consistent rule of law. Invest in deep counsel on issues of corporate governance and property protection rights.

Social responsibility will reach a new crescendo

Manufacturing excellence abounds in China, but it doesn't balance with public safety, environmental impact, and health risks. State-owned enterprises currently provide the majority of electrical power, and there is no pollution abatement. 30 percent of paper production waste water is recycled as compared to 80 percent in the United States and Europe. China has 5 out of the 10 most polluted cities in the world. Newspaper stories on the safety of food and food products are common, as are the efficacy issues facing pharmaceutical companies.

The Chinese struggle with how to use capital efficiently, guiding multinational companies to invest in improving the standard of living and employing more workers. Social responsibility initiatives to protect the environment and the food stream are not making the list. When environmental and social responsibility issues reach a crescendo during the Beijing 2008 Summer Olympics, large multinational companies, which spent more than $80 billion in China in 2005, will need to prepare to answer the larger social responsibility concerns of food and drug safety and environmental protection.

Protection of intellectual property

Remember when the Chinese were innovators? Marco Polo brought pasta to Italy from China, and the Chinese changed the face of civilization forever with the development of gunpowder and paper. The tables are now turned, with China excelling at borrowing from others (read: copying).

To understand the intellectual property issue, you must understand China. All private property was banned in China for decades. For centuries, all ideas have been owned by the state. The culture has no concept of protection of IP. According to some estimates, as much as a third of China's GDP comes from piracy and counterfeiting, including more than 90 percent of the country's software and 95 percent of its video games.

In *The Chinese Century: The Rising Chinese Economy and Its Impact on the Global Economy, the Balance of Power, and Your Job*, Oded Shenkar writes that five of six Yamaha motorcycles in China are fake. Perhaps this is because Yamaha's parts suppliers sell real Yamaha parts to fake Yamaha assemblers. The same goes for more than half of China's razor blades, cell phones, drugs, chewing gum, and shampoo. The streets are full of imitation; the Chinese are good at it.

In fact, technology absorption is far easier than innovation in China. Technology is everywhere. But while the Chinese love to use technology, it's ironic that the growing pool of talented people in China looking to innovate don't want to do it in their homeland.

Those heading to China should consider the country for the development part of R&D, but wait many years before placing bets on research. Pat Powers stated that it will take "at least 10 years to gain protection of intellectual property." In the meantime, companies can take their own measures by spreading production over multiple plants, with no one plant making the finished item, doing final fabrication in the market where the product is going to sell, and carefully controlling every step of high-value assembly with intellectual protection in mind.

The Chinese also generally have no appreciation for intangibles or royalties. Companies should structure trade knowing that they will never get payment on royalty rights.

Observations on navigating China's supply chain waters

No. 1—A huge consumer market is emerging, now 250 million strong.
While many customers in EMEA and North America recognize China as a critical link in the supply chain, few see it as an emerging market opportunity. China now has 250 million middle-class consumers—that's nearly the total population of the United States. It's not difficult to see how China is an immense market opportunity. The hard part is being first to market and building a sustainable brand.

No. 2—Supply chain experts are in short supply.
China has an official population of 1.3 billion, which makes it ironic that the largest limitation to supply chain management in China is people. By 2010, China will need an estimated 400,000 supply chain and logistics professionals, but Chinese universities produce only 10,000 logistics graduates each year.

Many cite the lack of middle management and professional supply chain managers as the greatest limitation to future growth. The lack of status is also an issue; positions in sales and civil service have far more status.

No. 3—For supply chain management, think basics.
For operations in China, focus on basics. The concepts of supply chain are beginning to form for leaders. Even warehouse management is spoken of as a multiyear implementation. The vice president of logistics for Shanghai Pharmaceuticals says that sharing information about demand limits supply chain management the most. The Chinese supply chain practice of demand sharing requires him to keep 40 days of inventory. He contrasted that with his experience in Japan, where he needed only 18 days of inventory, thanks to better visibility of demand.

No. 4—Visibility and transparency, not labor costs, are at the root of supply chain management.
Labor is a cost in North America and Europe, but not so in China. Employment goes hand in hand with growth. The low cost of labor in China allows companies to use extra bodies to sense and respond. As a result, the value proposition for supply chain management technology is not based on efficiency. Instead, it's visibility and channel transparency that speeds up trade.

No. 5—Logistics is a challenge, but not a permanent obstacle.
It currently takes nine days to move product from Shanghai to Urumqi—far too long, as one consumer products executive stated. However, it is changing with massive government investments. The plan is to have a new airport every 5 weeks for the next 10 years. In 2006, the government is investing $24 billion in the highway system and $42 billion in the rail network.

The larger issue—and one that will take awhile to change—is the fragmentation of the providers. Shanghai alone has 16,000 registered logistics companies. The largest single fleet comprises 3,000 trucks (Sinotrans). Trucking companies average 2.7 trucks. Imagine load tendering or lane optimization with this type of network.

The Greening
of the Supply Chain | 3

The Greening of the Supply Chain

Environmentalism is no longer about fringe elements living in trees—it's a mainstream concern. Increasingly, consumers are saving their green for green companies, and governments are responding to public pressure with new regulations to spur laggards along. Legislation in Europe, the United States, and even China is coming into force that is aimed at creating more environmentally friendly products and making companies accountable for their products long after they leave a store shelf.

While many companies see these as just more burdensome costs, the smart ones are jumping out ahead of the law and turning them into profits. They see not only the marketing potential in being green, but the efficiencies to be found in designing better from the get go and the profits to be made in taking ownership of their obsolete and used products.

In Chapter 3, we explore the various regulations now in effect, like RoHS and WEEE, and provide a new model for compliance that is helping companies find benefit in complying. There's also an interactive section to help companies evaluate their risk. We then offer case studies on companies that are going beyond the regulations and turning green into gold, and explore how the issue is becoming an executive- and board-level concern. Lastly, we look at the retail industry and its suppliers and how they are taking on their role at the front lines of the green movement.

How Green Is Your Supply Chain?

PART
ONE

Environmental compliance is a global trend. Worldwide, countries are introducing legislation that affects virtually all products at all levels of the supply chain.

The laws affect all aspects of business because they are rooted in cultural shifts that demand long-term protection for the earth and its inhabitants. Among the regulations companies have to navigate are the European Union's (EU) directives on Restriction of Hazardous Substances (RoHS), Waste Electrical and Electronic Equipment (WEEE), End-of-Life Vehicles (ELV), Packaging and Packaging Waste (The Essential Requirements) in the consumer products industry, and Registration, Evaluation, and Authorization of Chemicals (REACH) for the chemical industry (see Table 1).

It's not just the EU. China, Japan, and many states in the United States have been adopting similar laws that borrow the EU's text, in some cases passing even stricter legislation (see Part Three in this chapter for China's thorny RoHS). Expect more countries to follow.

Summary	Consumer Products	Automotive	Electronics	Chemicals
Directive	Packaging and Packaging Waste (The Essential Requirements)	End-of-Life Vehicles (ELV)	Waste Electrical and Electronic Equipment (WEEE)	Registration, Evaluation, and Authorization of Chemicals (REACH)
Date passed	March 1998	September 2000	January 2003	December 2005
Requirements	Packaging must be minimally subject to safety, hygiene, and consumer acceptance. Noxious or hazardous substances in packaging must be minimized and recoverable; they may be reusable. Statutory limits of heavy metals.	Reduce hazardous substances in product design. Facilitate dismantling, reuse, recovery, and recycling. Increase the use of recycled materials in vehicle manufacture. Ensure components do not contain hazardous substances.	Producers must set up systems for recovering electrical and electronic equipment. Also requires restricted use of certain hazardous substances in electrical and electronic equipment.	12,000 mass-produced chemicals need to be registered for every specific use and pass a series of requirements. According to the precautionary principle, a safety assessment based on testing results of the highest concern, chemicals will receive a five-year authorization.
When in effect	July 1998	April 2002	July 2004	Scheduled for end of 2007

Who it applies to	All packaging in EU market	Vehicle and material equipment manufacturers	Any organization that supplies electrical and/or electronic equipment to EU market	Entire chemical industry, with specific liabilities for manufacturers and importers
Materials/manufacturer responsibility	Responsibility varies by country—each has own directive plus regulations.	Original equipment manufacturers supply information about materials, parts, and systems that they manufacture and assemble (must engage supply chain). Suppliers must report on specific chemicals found in the materials, parts, and systems that they manufacture and assemble (flow from parts manufacturing to raw materials).	Producers will be responsible for taking back and recycling electrical and electronic equipment. This will provide incentives to design electrical and electronic equipment in a more environmentally efficient way, which takes waste management aspects fully into account.	Burden for registering is placed on the chemical manufacturers and importers, not the downstream users, such as formulators and brand owners.
How it is enforced	Tax based on material type, size, and weight	Enforced by each member state	Responsible for financing collection	To be determined

Table 1: Green regulations summary

Environmental compliance is reshaping the entire lifecycle of product development, from new requirements to end of life. For brand owners, the cost of noncompliance ranges from minor financial penalties to long-term brand erosion, and, in the extreme case, even jail time for negligent executives.

Entire product lines are subject to redesign, and individual products can be barred from sale to specific geographies. Just ask Sony about how much that can hurt. In late 2001, the Netherlands halted sales of PlayStations because they contained too much cadmium. The result: $110 million in lost revenue.

Creating a business case for environmental compliance includes risk factors and mitigation costs, but also provides opportunity to create competitive advantage. Consider the following:

- **Revenue risk**—Products sold into a region with environmental laws must be able to prove compliance or face having their entry barred. Further, manufacturing output can stall if needed parts are not available from the downstream supply chain.

- **Brand erosion**—If there are problems, the name on the product is going to get most of the bad press, for the most interesting story is the one that makes headlines. While Sony received all the headlines in the PlayStation example, it was a negligent supplier that supplied cadmium-laced cables against Sony's specifications.

- **Cost of compliance**—Depending upon the specific compliance initiative, the cost to mitigate can be between two and four percent of revenue for the first year, with long-term annual costs leveling off below one percent.

The cost of compliance

Compliance costs will vary, but here are some estimates:
- Various analyst estimates suggest ELV regulations could add $25 to $200 per vehicle in incremental costs.
- AMR Research estimates that the average cost of IT for supporting WEEE compliance ranges between $2 million and $3 million and will consume up to six percent of the IT development budget between 2003 and 2006.

- We also estimate that 50 to 75 percent of consumer goods final product costs are tied up in packaging, and that 80 percent of retailer supply chain cost is associated with the last 100 yards of getting a product to the shelf, requiring more store-ready packaging.
- REACH is estimated to cost the chemical industry $3 billion, with total economic costs estimated to range from less than $4 billion to more than $6 billion (with some estimates putting it up to $14 billion).

Responding to increasing regulation by retrofitting existing operations is a sure way to keep costs high without adding any benefit to the consumer. Consider the following:

- **Need to support multiple production lines**—Many companies will be forced to create a compliant production line while still running the noncompliant line in an effort to minimize lost revenue during the switch. A $1 billion consumer electronics company is spending $4 million to change a second line into a compliant one.

- **Excess and obsolete inventory**—Noncompliant inventory is often needed for product repairs, but many companies have long-term stockpiles that are headed for the waste pile. Alternatively, some companies will make last-time buys for hard-to-find noncompliant parts to avoid shortages. A midtier distributor recently threw away more than $6 million of inventory because of noncompliant goods.

- **Additional research and development**—Compliant products need to perform the same as their noncompliant counterparts. Changing component parts or formulas creates untested scenarios that need product and process redesign. A midtier consumer electronics company is spending more than $10 million in the first year for redesign and documentation.

- **Need for additional software**—Designers need enterprise systems that let them choose compliant components, support procurement systems, and produce reports. A large manufacturing company is examining two options: integrate an add-on module to its archaic system versus use this event as an opportunity to upgrade its entire product lifecycle management (PLM) system.

The model for product compliance

Executives understand the need for risk mitigation, but a barrage of metrics, facts, and opinions often paralyzes them. Most of the inputs simply confuse the issue, making it hard for executives to have the right information to make informed decisions. They need the AMR Research model for product compliance, which comprises two sections:
· A worksheet listing the major variables to determine a company's current compliance risk
· A listing of processes, concepts, and questions to mitigate exposure

The critical attributes to assess compliance preparedness fall into two categories: exposure and readiness (see Figure 1).

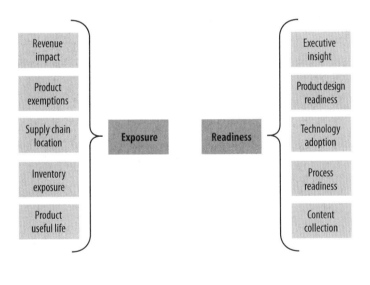

Figure 1: Assessment for environmental product compliance

Scored using a simple model of each attribute, the totals are plotted on a quadrant:

- **Proactive**—These companies have low exposure, yet are prepared. They will be able to adapt to changing regulations and obtain a competitive advantage.
- **Watch**—These are companies with high exposure, but they are also prepared. Because a significant amount of their business is affected by the regulation, they need to continually assess their readiness.
- **Prepare**—Companies with low exposure and low preparedness may feel that they are okay. However, because of rapidly changing regulations, they may move to the Trouble category.
- **Trouble**—Companies in this group need action plans immediately, as they have high exposure, yet they are not prepared. These companies will lose market share to companies in the Watch group as competitors exercise their advantages.

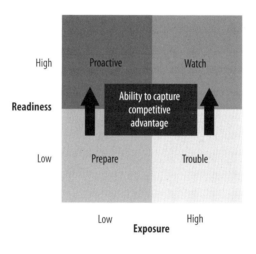

Figure 2: Environmental preparedness quadrants

73

The closer a company is to the top, the better it can capture competitive advantage as regulations change. Competitive advantage can come in the form of marketing to increase brand or exposing the weaknesses of competitors during the sales cycle. Regulations can also adapt by revising legal levels of hazardous materials. Companies that can access a rich database of information will be able to make changes with minimal effect, while competitors will have to spend significant money and time to prepare for the revision (more on this later).

Assessing exposure and readiness

This worksheet is generalized to fit all types of environmental compliance initiatives. It can be used by an individual company to assess its preparedness for a given regulation for a specific product line.

In using this tool, look at the attributes and choose 1 to 4, depending on the company's exposure and readiness. Then total and plot each score.

Exposure attributes

Revenue impact

If a company's products are not compliant with a country's specific regulations, it is at risk of being barred from sales, ultimately leading to lost revenue. On top of monetary problems, this also creates branding and market share concerns.

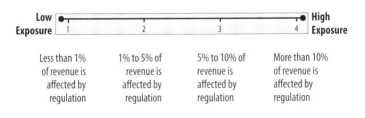

Low Exposure				High Exposure
1	2	3	4	
Less than 1% of revenue is affected by regulation	1% to 5% of revenue is affected by regulation	5% to 10% of revenue is affected by regulation	More than 10% of revenue is affected by regulation	

Product exemptions

Omissions and exemptions are frequent in compliance initiatives, such as for national infrastructure- or defense-related products. Technology exemptions create more exposure, though, because once a solution is found, the exemption disappears.

Low Exposure			High Exposure
1	2	3	4
All products are omitted from current regulations	Some products qualify for industry exemptions	Some products qualify for technology exemptions	No products qualify for exemptions

Supply chain location

The trend in environmental compliance is to move toward producer responsibility. This means that brand owners bear the responsibility and liability for compliance. Because brand owners will try to shift costs down the supply chain by only purchasing compliant products, all levels of the supply chain will be affected, but at less exposure than faced by the brand owners.

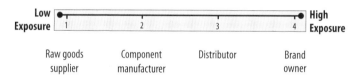

Low Exposure			High Exposure
1	2	3	4
Raw goods supplier	Component manufacturer	Distributor	Brand owner

Inventory exposure

Excess noncompliant inventory may have to be discarded. As dates move toward a specific environmental deadline, expect shortages of all products. End-of-life notices may spur an influx of last-time buys of noncompliant parts, and unknown demand for compliant parts will cause stockouts.

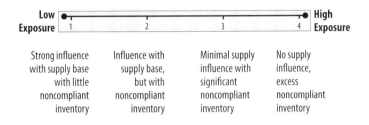

Low Exposure			High Exposure
1	2	3	4
Strong influence with supply base with little noncompliant inventory	Influence with supply base, but with noncompliant inventory	Minimal supply influence with significant noncompliant inventory	No supply influence, excess noncompliant inventory

Product useful life

Many environmental compliance initiatives require changes to components or formulas, which can change the use or create reliability concerns. Short-lifecycle products, such as cell phones, have less risk, as many producers have planned obsolescence strategies.

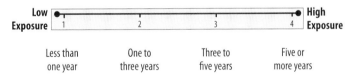

Low Exposure			High Exposure
1	2	3	4
Less than one year	One to three years	Three to five years	Five or more years

Calculate the total exposure by adding up the scores and dividing by five.

Exposure attributes	Score (1-4)	Low Exposure			High Exposure
Revenue impact		1	2	3	4
Product exemptions		1	2	3	4
Supply chain location		1	2	3	4
Inventory exposure		1	2	3	4
Product useful life		1	2	3	4
Exposure total					

Figure 3: Exposure attributes—results

Readiness attributes

Executive insight

Compliance becomes part of the culture of a company and the manner in which business is conducted. Without executive sponsorship, companies will not obtain the appropriate budget or authority to invest and adjust processes as needed.

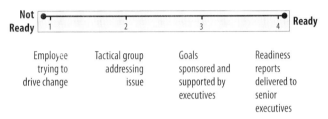

| Employee trying to drive change | Tactical group addressing issue | Goals sponsored and supported by executives | Readiness reports delivered to senior executives |

Product design readiness

Products on the market that do not adhere to the regulations need to be redesigned. This can become a significant effort, as all levels of the supply chain and product reliability may be affected.

| Products are not environmentally friendly | Designers have goals for environmental compliance | Products meet current environmental goals | Strategy to attain competitive advantage through proactive design compliance |

Technology adoption

In order to create compliant products and adapt to changing legislation, technology to aid design, procurement, and manufacturing is needed. Ultimately, robust reporting is needed to prove compliance.

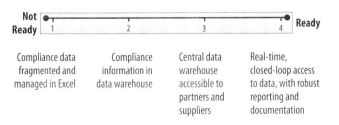

| Compliance data fragmented and managed in Excel | Compliance information in data warehouse | Central data warehouse accessible to partners and suppliers | Real-time, closed-loop access to data, with robust reporting and documentation |

Process readiness

Processes need to be examined and modified to ensure adherence to regulations. Examples of process modifications include part renumbering, supplier management, manufacturing processes, and repair management.

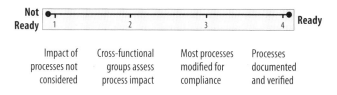

Not Ready				Ready
1	2	3	4	
Impact of processes not considered	Cross-functional groups assess process impact	Most processes modified for compliance	Processes documented and verified	

Content collection

Company strategies to collect information on products vary dramatically. Many simply collect a yes or no from the supplier that a part is compliant with a given regulation. Some try to collect the full material disclosure of every item, and therefore have the flexibility to adapt to changing and future regulations. The most proactive will verify the content with a third-party testing facility.

Not Ready				Ready
1	2	3	4	
Rely on supplier yes/no declaration for a specific regulation	Collect detailed data only for relevant compliance initiative	Comprehensive material declarations	Strategy to verify and assess component compliance	

Calculate the total readiness by adding up the scores and dividing by five.

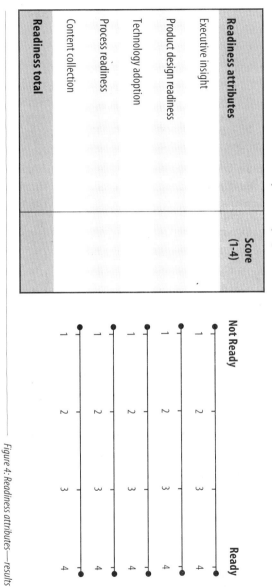

Readiness attributes	Score (1-4)
Executive insight	
Product design readiness	
Technology adoption	
Process readiness	
Content collection	
Readiness total	

Not Ready — **Ready**

Executive insight: 1 — 2 — 3 — 4

Product design readiness: 1 — 2 — 3 — 4

Technology adoption: 1 — 2 — 3 — 4

Process readiness: 1 — 2 — 3 — 4

Content collection: 1 — 2 — 3 — 4

Figure 4: Readiness attributes—results

Processes, concepts, and questions to prepare

Environmental regulations, while vast in scope, share many business requirements, allowing for a common approach and management. The environmental active compliance framework is an evolution of a financial model designed for compliance with the Sarbanes-Oxley Act (SOX).

Figure 5: Active compliance framework

81

This framework poses concepts and questions in the following categories:
- Policies and procedures
- Business processes, including business process management, supply chain management, production operations, and service lifecycle management
- Reporting and risk management
- Documents and records management
- Security and audit control

The content below should be used by executives to guide conversations. Where not all questions are relevant for every corporation or compliance event, they should all be considered.

Policies and procedures

Policies and procedures guide a corporation's compliance strategy. The following questions provide direction to the executive team, compliance group, and employees so that they can interact productively with regulatory bodies.

Long-term compliance

How much should you prepare for the future? Does your corporate culture address environmental concerns? Directives will change, and companies that are prepared will position themselves for long-term competitive advantage while preserving brand and avoiding costs.

Due diligence

How do you demonstrate compliance? Often directives only declare an end result (e.g., "less than x percent of a hazardous material can be present"), offering little leeway for interpretation of how companies should perform due diligence for the claim.

Product testing

How much should you test for performance? When substituting materials or changing processes for compliance, the end product changes, creating potential performance and reliability concerns. How much testing is enough?

Market choice

Is x percent of your revenue worth it? Companies that only do a small percentage of business in a highly restrictive foreign country may decide to treat that country's compliance as a lower priority.

Enforcement

When and how will the governments penalize? For new regulations, countries often delay penalties or do not enforce to the fullest extent. Alternatively, they may choose to make an example with harsh penalties to the first violator. What type of gamble are you willing to take?

Business processes

Business process management, supply chain management, production operations, and service lifecycle management all need to be assessed for compliance. Each of these processes needs to be evaluated by business group and the product lines within each group.

Business process management

· **New product introduction**—Will you alter the time frame for new product introductions? If so, how and when will the cutover occur? If not, will the delay reduce time-to-market benefits?

· **Product redesign**—What products need to be redesigned, and how will engineering account for the new compositions? Are compliant components available with the same characteristics, or does substantial redesign need to occur? How can products be redesigned to account for design for environment/disassembly/reuse?

· **Process redesign**—How will the newly designed products react in the manufacturing process, and how should that process change? What are the new test methods that ensure quality?

Supply chain management

· **Part renumbering**—Often compliant versus noncompliant parts have the same part numbers, depending on the supplier's strategy. How will you address part renumbering? How will you work with suppliers and customers to ensure the right product is ordered and shipped?

- **Inventory management**—How will new inventory affect your inventory management system? How will the shop floor change to accommodate multiple production lines?
- **Direct material sourcing**—How will you collect the homogeneous information about components in your products? How will last-time buys affect the supply?

Production operations
- **Quality management**—How will designed test methods be carried out in the production system? How will the results be captured and supplied back to the engineers?
- **Change management**—How will shop-floor change orders be captured, and what is the process for approval?
- **Manufacturing process planning**—How will designed processes be implemented from technology, production line, and employee perspectives?

Service lifecycle management
- **Field service communication**—What learning and tracking systems will be used to coordinate field service personnel's ability to repair compliant and noncompliant products?
- **Repair management**—What is the strategy to repair noncompliant products? How will you track backward compatibility or components? Can this as-serviced information get tracked back to the bill of materials?
- **Reverse logistics**—What will your strategy be to account for the end of product life? What technology will be used, and how will this be implemented? Will you be able to benefit from design for disassembly?

Reporting and risk management

Reporting is the main line of defense to manage the risks of noncompliance. Each channel provides different reporting requirements. While many reporting mandates and guidelines have yet to be agreed upon, companies must develop versatile competencies. The following are the relevant reporting channels.

Language management

The EU performs business in multiple languages. How will your company fill out necessary forms and produce reports as needed in foreign languages?

Local and national governments

Each government body may have its own forms and regulations to follow. Specific trade documents will need to pull data from multiple systems. Without these reports, companies may face market lockout, and they may not be able to create a reasonable defense if accused.

Business to consumer

Even for companies that do not sell directly to consumers, products may have detailed labeling requirements. How will these labels show compliance?

Business-to-business and distribution partners

Liability agreements between businesses and distribution partners are necessary to determine which company will accept risk. In a producer responsibility model, the default is the brand owner. That said, it is appropriate to shift responsibility for some distribution agreements and private labeling.

Recycling bodies

For discrete products, product disassembly and recovery instructions are often mandated. However, it is less clear how these instructions should be communicated. In addition, reporting between companies and government authorities may be necessary to track disposal and reclamation levels.

Document and records management

Documentation is critical to providing both management dashboard reports and a reasonable line of defense. The following are the top categories needed.

Supplier disclosures

Tracking multiple supplier responses and compliance activity is necessary and extremely difficult. The bar is raised higher because there is no consistent method of reporting, which overloads suppliers.

Registration

Compliance rules often dictate registration with the appropriate government body. Tracking the correspondence is necessary as different forms and information requests are made.

Exemption documentation

Exemptions have become a central focus of many companies. Documentation between regulatory bodies, companies, engineers, industries, and others must be tracked if any exemptions are to be declared.

Security and audit control

All compliance activity requires extensive security to guide and enforce a corporation's strategies and policies. The following are among the most critical controls.

Supplier monitoring

Auditing suppliers to ensure product declarations are accurate is a needed competency. Physical plant visits and component testing should be considered.

Product monitoring

Periodic testing by a third party of your entire product should be considered to protect against noncompliance accusations and support a reasonable defense.

Protection against renegade employees
Roles and access rights, along with audit logs, will allow only the appropriate people to make changes.

Customer and supplier access
Eventually, compliance should be pushed to customers and suppliers. This requires specific security provisioning.

Environmental compliance is a multi-industry, worldwide concern

While RoHS legislation is focused on the electronics industry, it actually borrows text from the ELV regulation, which aims to recover old vehicles. The chemical industry, meanwhile, is beginning to deal with the REACH directive, which puts the onus on producers to prove that certain chemicals are safe. Additional regulations affect batteries, all energy-using products, and packaging.

As environmental compliance initiatives dictate product requirements, companies need to continually assess their exposure and readiness. Beyond penalties, the risks include brand damage and revenue and market share loss. Smart companies will find ways to turn compliance into a competitive advantage, particularly as consumers increasingly look for the green in their brands.

Green Compliance: Yes, It's a Competitive Advantage

While all compliance creates legal obligations, environmental compliance raises the bar. Every state and country has different laws. Last year alone, 60 e-waste state laws were introduced in the United States.

But compliance shouldn't be looked at as a burden—it can be an opportunity for competitive advantage, as well. A quote in *The Wall Street Journal* by Benjamin Heineman, Jr., GE's former senior VP for law and public affairs, backs this sentiment: "… law and regulation, ironically, can be market enhancing because then all regulated entities face the same obligations under the law, and the smartest corporations will find a way to comply completely with imagination and less cost."

Environmental laws are market-changing events, creating opportunities for success—and opportunities for failure as well. A midtier component manufacturer recently lost a major customer because it couldn't articulate its compliance strategy. The competitor that won the business highlights its green strategy on its first slide during presentations.

89

Finding green in the complexity

Here's the complexity facing global companies: they must understand applicable regulations, multiply them by every geography in which they do business, then define the different types of processes and technology considerations with which to comply, weighing all of that against customer-specific regulations.

If environmental regulation costs manufacturers one to two percent of revenue, what will they get in return? The answer is nothing if compliance is tacked on without revisiting assumptions about how products are designed, built, and delivered. As stated in the Directive on Packaging and Packaging Waste, "the Technical Committee TC261/SC4 on Packaging and the Environment opted for a management system approach aimed at ensuring a continuous effort to improve." No one is going to jail, but winners will be those that embrace the spirit, not just the letter, of the law and use that to their advantage.

Those that comply reactively will spend money on returns logistics, manual materials identification and tracking, and reporting. As regulations tighten over time, these costs are likely to grow geometrically, as added layers of responsibility multiply operations and information integration complexity. Those that comply proactively and design out wasteful product costs in the supply chain will spend money on product and manufacturing process design, supplier collaboration, and material specification systems. As new rules come into effect, they will be better able to comply with less added costs to direct materials and conversion operations (see Table 2).

To repeat Mr. Heineman, the smartest corporations will find a way to comply completely with imagination and less cost.

Steps	Reactive	Proactive
Approach	Wait for regulations to be defined and enforced	Anticipate regulation and analyze product design implications
Actions	Build supply chain to handle returns and recycling	Establish design for supply chain program extending to end of life
	Build information systems to support returns supply chain	Measure material composition and assembly complexity
Costs	Logistics, new tooling and equipment, manual data cleansing, and reporting and document distribution; increasing with growing rules	Education, enhanced CAD/product data management, specification management systems, and new tooling and equipment
Timing	Later, as regulations take effect	Now, as budget cycles permit
Other benefits	None	Lower direct material costs, conversion costs, and service and warranty expenses

Table 2: Green compliance strategies

So where are the opportunities?

Here are some highlights:

- **Branding**—GE, with its $1.5 billion spending on ecomagination, is addressing its questionable past and transforming itself into an environmental player.

- **New service offerings**—IBM's multibillion-dollar GARS unit collects 20,000 end-of-lease machines each week and then resells, refurbishes, and dismantles them, contributing less than two percent to landfill.

- **Product redesign**—Sun's CoolThreads technology increases the performance of its servers fivefold while reducing energy consumption, thus creating a return on investment for its customers.

- **Product initial design**—In its Parametric Car enterprise design program, BMW mandates that full lifecycle environmental impact analysis is fundamental to all new vehicle programs as part of overall cost planning. And a packaging engineer at a respected global consumer goods manufacturer defines its company's principles in terms of cost: "The goal is to eliminate packaging in the first place."

- **Enhancing relationships**—Fujitsu Transaction Systems uses environmental regulations as an opportunity to educate and solidify relationships with its customer base, effectively turning it into a trusted advisor rather than simply a supplier.

- **Internal infrastructure**—In preparation for ELV, a Tier 1 automotive supplier significantly updated its processes and enabling technology. Its spending for RoHS regulations is less than one percent of revenue, where companies of similar size are spending between two and four percent.

Simply put, proactive compliance with environmental regulation is inseparable from principles of design for supply chain.

True best practice is exemplified by the case of Grundfos, a $2.2 billion Denmark-based manufacturer of pumps. Commanding a 50 percent world market share of the circulator pumps that drive heating, ventilation, and air conditioning equipment, the company estimates that its products consume five percent of global electricity production annually. The environmental impact of these products is so dramatic that Grundfos is not only certified under the ISO 14001 International Environmental Standard, but goes so far as to make sustainability the first goal cited by group president Niels Due Jensen in the company's annual report.

Although only minimally affected by directives like WEEE, Grundfos anticipates green regulations for things like variable speed requirements on its pumps. The intention of such rules would be to improve fuel efficiency. To Grundfos, this might mean new business and an even wider advantage against competitors.

These examples are typical of organizations that see environmental regulation as the logical complement to a design for supply chain philosophy. In automotive, for instance, full lifecycle parametric modeling of vehicles contributes to understanding manufacturing and assembly steps to reduce production costs and streamline disassembly and recovery of materials at end of life. Best-in-class materials or part specification systems have been shown to reduce direct material costs by as much as five percent in consumer packaged goods and electronics. This same system is the essential ingredient for complying with WEEE and RoHS.

Blue-chip companies are taking notice and producing sustainability reports. Often more than 50 pages long, these annual reports detail their strategies to address environmental and other social concerns. The Global Reporting Initiative (GRI), which collects corporate sustainability reports, has more than 800 global companies in its database, including Dell, Ford, Matsushita, McDonald's, Nike, and Starbucks. People can argue about the merits of GE's environmental posture, but few can argue that it is taking a sensitive topic and finding ways to capitalize and enhance its brand.

Compliance Is Also an Executive Problem

Any company doing business in the EU will have to comply with the WEEE, RoHS, and REACH directives. Those selling electronics into China will soon have to comply with the country's even stricter restrictions.

Not meeting these directives could cost companies millions. They must be an executive-level priority. Environmental compliance risks are being managed too low in the organization, risking significant revenue opportunities, increasing costs, and destroying brand image.

Deadlines are looming

The deadline for RoHS is July 1, 2006. By that date, all nonmilitary products will need to be void of lead, mercury, cadmium, and other harmful substances. For the EU, simply shipping product after the date declares compliance, but detailed documentation will be needed if questioned by authorities.

For WEEE, all EU countries were to have transposed the directive into law by August 13, 2005. However, only a handful has by mid 2006. To comply, companies will need to register products and finance the collection and recycling of roughly 75 percent of products.

Getting the lead out

Lead is proving to be the most notable substance banned under RoHS. The problem is that lead is very useful in electronics: it is a conductive metal, relatively inexpensive, has a low melting point, and, most importantly, helps prevent a phenomenon known as "whiskering." Tin whiskers (tin is especially prone, thus the name) are small, electrically conductive strands that grow on various metals and have caused more than $1 billion worth of premature product failures. As the whiskers grow, they can cause short circuits. The problem: there is no known cure other than lead.

Expensive whisker-related failures are well documented: satellites, Patriot missiles, pacemakers, and computer equipment have all failed because of the problem. In fact, it is among the chief reasons why military equipment and medical devices are exempt from RoHS requirements. Other electronics products, however, do need to be compliant. HP and Sony are among the high-profile companies looking for exemptions. Both companies want a small percentage of lead to stay in the manufacturing process for certain products.

Most companies, however, will need to design their products differently. The following technology can help them get the lead out:
- *Product portfolio management applications can help quantify risk across a collection of products.*
- *Collaborative product design applications can help diverse groups comment on designs and build internal sets of best practices.*
- *Existing product data management applications can help track supplier practices.*
- *Integrating with a customer relationship management system to obtain end-user feedback will yield pertinent information (along with other product development feedback).*

RoHS is a huge issue, so why is it being handled so far down in the company?

Every company in the electronics supply chain, from parts manufacturers to retail outlets, needs to have strategies to comply with these EU regulations. Right now, the wrong questions are often being asked by the wrong people in the development of these strategies. Employees from environmental health and safety and parts procurement teams are discerning how to substitute for lead in their products. While this is important to understand, executives need to be asking bigger questions:

· How much revenue is at risk?
· How long will it take to fix the problem?
· How much will it cost?
· What parts and products are affected?
· How do the regulations vary from country to country?

OEMs are leading the way in RoHS denial

Original equipment manufacturers (OEMs) are telling suppliers to deal with the problem. Unfortunately, the suppliers' razor-thin margins have already been stretched. Shortages of compliant parts and confusion over part numbers are certain. OEMs cannot define the impact of the problem and therefore cannot state if it is a material impact.

RoHS: an industry breakdown

Consumer electronics

RoHS is aimed directly at the consumer electronics industry. Because of the rate of innovation and the business models based on planned obsolescence, electronic products are ending up in landfills at unprecedented rates. While large, midsize, and small consumer electronics companies face similar exposures, the companies are markedly different in their preparation. The most important measure is the knowledge and involvement of the executives. Many large companies have RoHS task forces in place, made up of multidisciplinary groups of people that report to a senior executive. Large companies have long understood the exposure and have invested in the technology and processes, but the naiveté of smaller businesses in general is alarming. Many have yet to define a formal strategy for compliance and lack the infrastructure to address the issues in a timely manner.

White goods

White goods producers have higher exposure to RoHS than consumer electronics manufacturers because of product longevity. Refrigerators and washing machines, for instance, are intended to last a long time, creating a necessity for exhaustive product testing. If a white goods product fails after a few years, it could hurt the brand. Companies in the market, however, are not prepared. With so much focus on consumer electronics, many industry participants are unaware of the regulations and are not ready.

Aerospace and defense

Claiming industry exemptions, A&D companies have little immediate exposure to RoHS. They are still at risk, however, because specific components become unavailable in the supply chain because of product phaseouts.

WEEE could be a logistics nightmare

While RoHS states that harmful substances cannot go into products, WEEE makes companies accountable for the recovery of waste. This reverse procurement concern is forcing producers to finance the collection, treatment, recycling, and recovery of electronics waste. This creates an unbelievable logistics challenge and opens up new markets to those in waste and transportation businesses.

WEEE demands executives ask the right questions:
· How much will this cost?
· What are the brand repercussions of noncompliance? (Producers will be contacting the consumer in new ways.)
· How can the company encourage (or force) consumers to return products?
· What partnerships need to be in place?

Chemical reaction REACHes boiling point

Meanwhile, the chemical industry's REACH directive, which starts sometime in 2006–2007 and extends out for the following 11 years, intends to account for the roughly 30,000 chemicals used in the EU. The primary goal is to reduce the amount of hazardous chemicals in the environment while also limiting animal testing. It will require all mass-produced chemicals (greater than one metric ton) be registered for every specific use. Dangerous chemicals will be evaluated after they pass a series of requirements in which companies will be forced to share testing data. Chemicals that are deemed safe will receive a five-year authorization.

With cost to the chemical industry at $3 billion and total economic costs estimated at between less than $4 billion and more than $6 billion (with some estimates putting it up to $14 billion), businesses are being levied with a heavy burden. The excessive costs will put many small and midsize businesses out of business, a particularly troublesome reality for the highly fractured chemical industry.

Currently 1,000 pages, but estimated to grow to approximately 15,000 pages, REACH is a massively complex piece of legislation. It will continue to grow in intricacy as each EU member state transposes it into law, compounded by language barriers and cultural desires. It does not take a chemical engineer to see that litigation will create the case law that will ultimately determine the real rules for REACH.

Not only will these issues not go away, they will get worse. It is possible that WEEE and RoHS will add additional hazardous products, change minimum tolerances, and modify recovery rates. New regulations will continue to surface as more countries become green and pose their own set of compliance hurdles.

China RoHS is thornier than EU RoHS

China, for one, is getting ready to implement its own version of RoHS, which will have many more strenuous implications for those affected. China's flavor of RoHS, "Administrative Measure on the Control of Pollution Caused by Electronic Information Products," is more inclusive, requires product marking, and will ultimately require certification. In short, the Chinese are enacting a stringent law that raises the bar to comply, especially for foreign companies.

Innocent until proven guilty or guilty until proven innocent?

To declare compliance for EU RoHS, those selling product into member states simply ship product. No markings are required, nor is documentation needed for entry. In fact, little information exists on what constitutes appropriate due diligence, and there is little insight about penalties. In essence, companies are innocent until proven guilty.

Not so in China. Beginning March 1, 2007, products need specific marking. China suggests that, sometime in the future, state-owned laboratories will certify whether products are compliant before they can be sold. This guilty until proven innocent foundation creates an advantage for Chinese companies.

Here is a sampling of reasons why Chinese companies will have the advantage:

- All enlisted products need a 3C label (China Compulsory Certification) before they can be sold in China, but a number of Chinese electronic manufacturers have this certification already.
- Testing for the ultimate certification will likely be allowed only at state-owned, approved laboratories. Time to market will be a problem because the amount of products needing certification will greatly outweigh the capacity available. If a western company and a Chinese company each need products certified, which one do you think will be prioritized?
- Neither the law, nor supplemental material, is translated into other languages. Officials decided to only publish information in Chinese, which creates significant time and information barriers for small and midsize businesses, though "unofficial" third-party translations can be found on the web.

Take a deep breath. Talk with suppliers, customers, and vendors. Act quickly.

Prudent organizations have a number of steps they can and should undertake immediately:

- Assess your company's exposure given these new requirements and evaluate readiness. Ultimately it will allow your company to comply and find competitive advantage.
- Find out if your products require certification. The EU defined eight categories of electrical and electronic equipment, but offers exemptions to certain products. China starts with a blank category, and then adds products that can be made environmentally safe using current technology, so there's no exemptions. The amount of products will likely expand through time.
- Work with your Chinese counterparts. Use the knowledge and insider advantage of your Chinese subsidiary, manufacturing plant, or partners.
- Adopt standards. Work with your supplier and customer bases to adopt the IPC1752 standard for declaring materials.

Is China becoming sympathetic to global sustainability issues? Doubtful. However, it does realize that forcing industries to deal with environmental concerns will make it more competitive against the United States and other countries, further propelling it to join the dominant players of the world economy.

Greening of Retail

PART
FOUR

When it comes to a green supply chain, retailers are the front line—in direct contact with the end consumers leading the green movement.

When a manufacturer has a shaky environmental record, it's the retailer that will first feel public backlash. But it's not just reactionary either. With its unparalleled influence on consumer buying habits, no other industry has more power to change the environmental and social makeup of the world for the better. As such, retailers, at an increasing rate, are creating sustainable business models, ones that are not only fiscally responsible, but are equally socially and environmentally aware.

While many retailers are creating sustainable business models and reaping the rewards, there is still a long way to go. Out of 831 companies registered in the Global Reporting Initiative's global reporting database, only 30 are retailers. The database is a tally of companies that have released reports on their use of the GRI's sustainability guidelines. These guidelines are "for voluntary use by organizations for reporting on the economic, environmental, and social dimensions of their activities, products, and services. The aim of the guidelines is to assist reporting organizations and their stakeholders in articulating and understanding contributions of the reporting organizations to sustainable development." Among the retailers listed are global names like Carrefour, H&M, Marks & Spencer, McDonald's, Metro Group, Safeway, and Starbucks.

To join the green revolution, retailers can implement simple changes, such as using recycled bags, decreasing circulars and direct mail, and using earth-friendly cleaning products—but so much more can be done. Some are advancing strategic initiatives that are not only conscientious, but boost customer loyalty and improve margin at the same time: making money and saving the world. Meeting minimum government and industry standards may help avoid bad publicity, but smart retailers will distinguish their brand and generate revenue and profits by employing the following practical social and environmental strategies.

No. 1: Make recycling products easy

Consumers want to properly dispose of environmentally hazardous products, especially obsolete consumer electronics, but they don't want to work for it. Regrettably, most retailers and manufacturers don't effectively promote the process and provide incentives. Now some manufacturers like IBM, HP, Dell, and Nike, as well as retailers like Office Depot and Staples, are trying to buck the trend, making it easy (and profitable) to recycle batteries, computers, sneakers, and ink cartridges. For the retailers, this brings customers into the stores to receive recycling/purchasing incentives.

Office Depot and HP recently partnered to pilot the first free, nationwide, in-store electronics recycling program in the United States. The program collected 10.5 million pounds of products from 200,000 customers and transported it to one of HP's U.S. recycling facilities. IBM, meanwhile, has established the Asset Recovery Center in Endicott, New York, which demanufactures and scraps 28 million pounds of equipment, producing 1.5 million usable parts that are resold. In 2003, IBM said it sold more than $1.5 billion of used equipment. While this is mostly from leased equipment and not retail sales, it's environmentally friendly and profitable. More than 98 percent of this volume in the demanufacturing process is recycled, with less than two percent of the materials sent to landfills.

For its part, Nike began collecting worn-out athletic shoes (of any brand) in 1993 and turned them into a secondary business. The shoes are broken down into three materials—Nike Grind Rubber (goes into baseball and soccer fields, golf products, weight room flooring, and running tracks), Nike Grind Foam (used in synthetic basketball courts, tennis courts, and playground surfaces), and Nike Grind Upper Fabric (from textile and leather uppers, and used for padding under hardwood basketball floors)—that are used by a number of independent manufacturers to create the various sports surfaces. Nike also donates some of the material to build sports surfaces for underserved areas around the world.

The takeback program established needs to be developed based on a joint value proposition, one in which all parties benefit: the consumer gains easy disposal and gets credit for it (Office Depot and HP were giving consumers a free package of recycled printer paper for every empty ink cartridge they returned), and the retailer and manufacturer benefit from operationally efficient processes for reverse logistics and remanufacturing.

Companies also gain in customer loyalty and bigger sales. Office Depot reported a rise in customer traffic during the pilot with HP, and every consumer that comes to the store to return an empty ink cartridge is one that Office Depot can turn into more sales. Both companies also benefit from advertising what happens to those cartridges and electronics. The cartridges aren't just being refilled or dumped in a landfill, but are instead turned into shoe soles, serving trays, fence posts, and—yes—other HP products, like scanners. The electronics, from laptops and PDAs to printers, are also finding new life as everything from airplane parts to little red wagons.

No. 2—Implement green logistics (and slash costs)

With fewer truck drivers earning more because of demand, not to mention skyrocketing insurance and fuel costs, transportation has become a larger drain on operational expenses. Meanwhile, retailers must comply with new Environmental Protection Agency (EPA) regulations to improve overall air quality, which translates into more costs. Several large retailers and carriers are testing oil purification technology from companies such as Oil Purification Systems to improve oil quality—extending the life of the engine, cutting down on oil consumption, and reducing the amount of potentially harmful oil for waste disposal.

Consumers are also becoming increasingly aware of green vehicles as the growing demand for hybrid vehicles spills over into other areas. In fact, in some political races (the 2006 Massachusetts governor's race, for instance), how gas-guzzling the candidates' cars are has become a political issue. It's only a matter of time before it spreads to consumer-facing companies where transportation is their brand: think Zipcar, FedEx, and Peapod.

These companies should invest more in hybrid vehicles that will not only save on gas (which translates into bottom-line savings), but show the world that their brand is conscious of the environment.

UPS is on that road. The company spent more than $2.1 billion on fuel last year, which is about 4.8 percent of its operating budget, Mike Herr, the shipping giant's vice president of environmental affairs, recently told *Forbes*. As part of its ongoing search for ways to cut those costs (and help the environment in the process), UPS recently ordered 50 hybrid trucks for its fleet. The company wins, the environment wins, and, if marketed well, customers could be enticed to use UPS over the competition.

No. 3—Develop environmentally sensitive products

As private-label products become a larger percentage of the overall assortment for grocery, apparel, consumer electronics, and general merchandise retailers, these retailers should be thinking more about the green components and packaging. Like the organic section in a supermarket, don't be surprised to see green products as a category within clothing, electronic, and other types of stores. These products are often what draw consumers to specialty stores like REI, Trader Joe's, and Whole Foods. Expanding a product line may attract a new demographic, not to mention the additional opportunity to grab market share if companies can find a way to make organic food, clothes, and cleaning products more affordable.

And don't forget labeling. Clearly labeling ingredients, whether mandated or not, will build consumer loyalty.

No. 4—Ensure supplier code of ethics

For retailers, global manufacturing and supply chains make it difficult to monitor and audit supplier partners to ensure they are being socially responsible to the environment and to the workers in manufacturing facilities. (Remember the Kathy Lee Gifford clothing line scandal?) Retailers must establish processes and visibility to ensure manufacturers are operating above board. This will help avoid noncompliance fines and embarrassing press, which can be even more costly. Clothing retailer American Eagle, which caters to the increasingly green-conscious youth market, established what it calls a supply chain performance program to address this issue. It enhances internal and external collaboration and ensures that supplier operations and products meet social compliance requirements and supply chain security policies.

Responsible sourcing

Retailers are on the front lines of the responsible sourcing wars. When it was reported that Kathy Lee Gifford's clothing line was being manufactured by child labor overseas, the reputation of the retailer selling her goods was also at stake. Many of the retailers have policies in place demanding fair labor practices and environmentally sound manufacturing, but have still been caught off guard because they weren't monitoring contractors and subcontractors. A number of them are now enlisting various programs to help combat these issues. In 1995, The Gap began letting independent monitors evaluate its factories in Central America, becoming the first U.S. apparel company to do so.

Others are signing on to programs like the European Ethical Trading Initiative (ETI). Under ETI, a company assumes responsibility for labor and human rights practices within its supply chain. ETI has 37 retail and supplier companies, 16 nongovernmental organizations, and 3 international trade union secretariats. Its base code is as follows:

- *Employment is freely chosen.*
- *Freedom of association and collective bargaining are rights.*
- *Working conditions are safe and hygienic.*
- *Child labor shall not be used.*
- *Living wages are paid.*
- *Working hours are not excessive.*
- *No discrimination is practiced.*
- *Regular employment is provided.*
- *No harsh or inhumane treatment is tolerated.*

ETI members have made public commitments to labor standards, verifying compliance and reporting results to stakeholders.

Companies are also setting up and more diligently enforcing supplier guidelines that include social and environmental requirements, supplier codes of conduct, and complete supplier requirements and assessments. In fact, responsible sourcing is becoming a part of the supplier award equation. The preferred suppliers have traditionally been viewed as those with the best performance, total cost, quality, and product/process innovation. In leading-edge companies, corporate social responsibility is now part of the preferred supplier equation, ensuring social and environmental compliance as well. The suppliers that qualify have solid policies and practices in place and have been audited and tested by their customers. The expectations for these suppliers and the scorecard requirements have now changed based on corporate social responsibility in sourcing.

No. 5—Eliminate paper from operations

Paper clutters store operations. Whether in the form of receipts, coupons, training materials, or task checklists, retailers waste tons of paper. To reduce waste, home improvement retailer B&Q removed 2,000 pages of paper per store per week by implementing electronic workflows for store communications. The UK-based retailer not only significantly reduced paper, but it also enhanced operations transparency, ensuring that stores accurately and effectively executed all assigned tasks.

Other retailers, including Smart&Final and Circuit City, are digitizing receipts and creating online access to order and account information. Digital receipts have created easier returns processing, reduced shrink, and satisfied more customers. Not only do they save money on paper, but automated processes streamline operations and increase employee efficiency, which ultimately leads to increased sales and a better shopping experience.

No. 6—Use alternative sources of energy

The amount of energy U.S. retailers consumes is off the charts. Most people forget to turn off the lights after leaving a room in their own house, so it's hard to expect store associates to be energy conscious when they aren't even paying the bill. Retailers such as Food Lion, however, have made energy efficiency part of their corporate culture.

Along with earning the Energy Star Sustained Excellence 2006 Award from the EPA, Food Lion is an active participant in the new Energy Efficiency Leadership Group. It will help develop and document sound business practices for energy efficiency, agreeing to pursue these practices through its business channels upon completion.

On the other side of the pond, UK-based Tesco is deploying clear roofs to maximize natural light and passive heating and cooling mechanisms. The firm anticipates cutting in half by 2010 the amount of energy used in stores compared with consumption in 2000. Those energy savings translate into bottom-line savings.

Get credit for being green

Stand out as a company that cares and increase customer loyalty and profits in the process. Implement these strategies because they are good for business, and let consumers know. Being green is a marketing opportunity—promote green culture via websites, signage, press, and associates. In today's world, being environmentally and socially conscious is a selling point, not a cost. And that translates into profit, as companies like Nike, HP, and IBM have learned.

Look for opportunities in-store and throughout the supply chain to have social and environmental responsibility permeate the organization. Store associates are a huge extension of brand, and only when they understand the corporation's stance regarding green can they communicate the brand position and act within social responsibility guidelines.

Also know the customers: what are their concerns and priorities? Understand their collective thoughts and then craft messages and marketing programs accordingly. Apply this to merchandising, product designers, and marketing teams, and have them discuss opportunities to create messages. Know what development and supply chain investments are taking place, and figure out how they can be branded or capitalized on to demonstrate competitive advantage. Then incorporate all of this into the business plan.

Supplying Health | 4

Supplying Health

Pharmaceutical, medical device, and healthcare services remain a pain point for economies around the world. Developing nations cannot afford the latest technologies and thus suffer from persistent health crises, while developed-world economies face fast-rising costs that threaten basic competitiveness with ever higher social costs.

Productivity gains in other supply-chain-intensive industries have shown the potential for healthcare to make huge strides in the wider provision of basic supplies and greater cost efficiency. The major issues are learning to accelerate product development while operating under massive and growing regulatory burdens and finding ways to streamline inventory management and replenishment systems without compromising patient safety.

In Chapter 4, we explore how profitable growth can be achieved with the application of operational excellence principles combined with tighter new product development processes. We also offer insight into the role of supply chain in tackling crises like the avian flu threat.

Fixing Healthcare To Fix Health

*Heightened competition, increased generic drug production,
and pressure from managed care and government agencies
(as well as the public) to curb costs and meet the needs of
underserved areas are all converging on the pharmaceutical
and life sciences industries. This new reality is threatening
the decades of growth they have enjoyed.*

Further exacerbating the problem is the fact that these industries are still plagued by poor operational performance, a legacy of the days of high margins and low cost of goods sold.

Pharmaceutical and life sciences companies may not have seen the implications of this weakness in the past, but with compliance, competition, expiring patents, and pipeline and commercial growth issues, manufacturing and product supply excellence is emerging as a cornerstone strategy for the future. If these companies are going to meet the health needs of the world while remaining profitable, they need to first fix their own ailing processes and structures.

Growth, operations, and compliance: the challenges

The complexity and deep science basis of drugs, sophisticated medical devices, and delivery mechanisms have made it difficult for pharmaceutical and life sciences companies to increase profitability while developing new products, needing as they do to balance supply and demand while meeting tougher regulatory standards. Figure 1 examines how the current business environment is addressed through critical business strategies and technology.

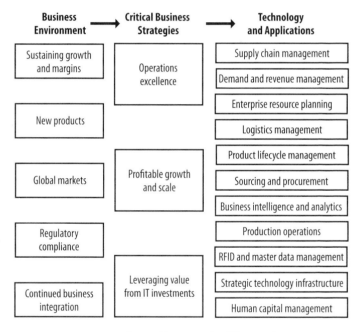

Figure 1: Pharmaceutical and life sciences business environment

Sustaining growth and margins

The push to reduce healthcare costs is putting pressure on the high margins traditionally enjoyed by the industry. Pharmaceutical manufacturers continue to struggle with inefficiencies, including high inventory levels and cycle time waste in the existing product supply model. Even with total inventories as high as 200 to 300 days, 7 to 10 percent stockout rates persist—a bane to the bottom line. Compare this to the consumer products industry, in which inventory management has slashed total inventory to 60 to 70 days with minimal stockouts.

As pressure on productivity and costs increases, manufacturers are moving to demand-driven business models to help ease the pain. Much like consumer products manufacturers are instituting demand-driven supply network (DDSN) strategies based on consumer demand, pharmaceutical and life sciences firms are doing the same, except that the mechanics for the moment of truth—when a customer looks for a product—are different. Where product availability and usage dominates in consumer products, the moment of truth in life sciences is about a consumer-centered flow of safe products.

New products

Faced with organizational and investor demand to grow and a portfolio of expiring patents, companies look to new products to fuel future growth. However, the complexity, testing, and regulatory demands of pharmaceutical and life sciences products result in an extended and expensive new product development process. For example, the cost of a new molecular entity (a drug based on new chemicals acting in new ways to treat a disease) is more than $800 million. The time for an investigational new drug (IND)—the status the Food and Drug Administration (FDA) gives to a new drug that is ready to be tested on people—to market is 8 to 10 years, with less than 20 percent of INDs for new molecular entities making it to the final new drug approval stage: the application to the FDA for a license to the sell the drug. With such high costs, drug companies are dropping compounds that exhibit a marginal probability of success before they enter clinical trials. Unsurprisingly, the number of new drug approvals to the FDA has declined the past few years, while the number of biotech and big pharmaceutical collaborations and partnering has grown considerably, with more than $17 billion in deals in 2005.

The global landscape for research and development has also changed. European companies have relocated a large number of facilities and researchers to the United States because of the more favorable governmental policies and attitudes toward biopharmaceutical research. The high costs are also changing the focus of R&D. More efforts are concentrated on products for chronic rather than acute diseases, with the top pharmaceutical R&D dollars going to the anticancer, neurological, anti-infective, and metabolic therapeutic classes.

In order to cut the time to market, companies are starting to foster a closer relationship between their R&D and manufacturing functions. In leading companies, technology architects are building a process language that facilitates a design-to-manufacture process in order to exchange information between the highly separated functions of R&D and manufacturing. The same approach has been taken in other industries, where better product lifecycle management (PLM) tools and processes have successfully cut time to market by 50 to 70 percent. The lessons learned are transferable, as everything from chemical formula definition to materials engineering has benefited from software applications that better tie a designer's intent to the manufacturing or sourcing implication.

FDA + big pharma + PLM = better healthcare for all

Members of the pharmaceutical and life sciences industries say that a meaningful partnership with the FDA can be formed to bring technology and best practices to bear for faster and more effective new drug discovery and industrialization. The catalyst is the FDA's Critical Path Initiative, championed by Dr. Janet Woodcock, the agency's then director for the Center for Drug Evaluation and Research (and now deputy director of FDA operations), which aims to "modernize the techniques and methods used to evaluate the safety, efficacy, and quality of medical products as they move from product selection and design to mass manufacture." At its heart is the FDA's attempt to move away from a policing role and toward a more facilitative coaching role.

Skepticism persists, however, especially on how effectively central mandates and policy statements on the Critical Path Initiative can be pushed down to the field investigator level. Yet agreement on fundamental trends suggests the weight of common sense will win out over bureaucratic inertia. The average cost of new drug development has crossed the $1 billion mark, with multiyear development cycles placing huge financial risks on big pharma companies as they search for the next blockbuster. Current FDA procedures only add to the bill. Consider the possibility of a thousand configurations on a thousand new drugs. Personalized medicine is scientifically possible and very compelling from a public health standpoint, but current FDA procedures can't handle the volume. Something has to give.

Lastly, 50 percent faster and cheaper to market is possible with PLM technology and best practices. They are proven to cut product development, launch time, and cost by that much in other industries. Drug maker AstraZeneca has presented its success and huge gains in financial and resource efficiency using PLM tools, namely modeling applications.

The Critical Path Initiative provides the rallying cry for FDA-pharmaceutical industry collaboration to make healthcare products cheaper and more widely available. The technology and best practice foundations have been laid by industries from automotive to electronics, and early results are convincing. For innovation in life sciences to realize its potential for public health and corporate profits, PLM tools and lessons must be harnessed to ramp up new drugs with quality designed and built in from the beginning rather than tacked on via inspection at the end.

119

Global markets

As growing economies like China and India stabilize, opportunities are created for low-cost manufacturing and worldwide product sourcing. This also adds risk as supply chains are extended and intellectual property (IP) management becomes more difficult. Global pharmaceutical companies are investing heavily in countries like China, with investments in R&D as a priority. Companies like Wyeth, GlaxoSmithKline, and Novartis are taking advantage of large pools of inexpensive local talent by establishing development centers in these regions. Many industries are struggling with protecting IP in outsourced innovation and China-based sourcing, and the lessons learned are very much applicable to life sciences.

Manufacturers also see great selling opportunities in these developing markets. As branded drugs are manufactured in these regions, they will become cheaper and compete with locally produced generics and traditional medicine. The large aging population and rapid economic growth in many regions make these promising markets for pharmaceutical and life sciences companies. However, weak patent protection laws, the high cost of drug distribution, and government pricing are still significant barriers. Still, overcoming these barriers is not impossible, as consumer products companies like P&G and Unilever are demonstrating today in sub-Saharan Africa.

Regulatory compliance

The FDA, Securities and Exchange Commission (SEC), and Environmental Protection Agency (EPA) have imposed rules and regulations on the way manufacturers must operate. Compounding these regulatory demands are the different departments and sites within a business that are responsible for various aspects of the enforcement of regulatory rules and regulations. The compliance execution differences, gaps, and duplication across departments and sites have added cycle times, risk, and cost to operations. Companies need to start organizing for these new realities (see Chapter 2 for more).

Pharmaceutical and life sciences executive leadership teams do not typically regard manufacturing and supply chain abilities as huge strategic risks, but recent events clearly show how quality and compliance can quickly cause acquisitions or a product launch to fail. The folly is thinking of compliance as merely a cost instead of a means to improve business performance. The irony is that even with the flurry of regulatory-driven spending in IT and focus on operations excellence, applications such as manufacturing execution, laboratory information management, and corrective and preventive action systems still tend to be bolted-on components. This results in a fragmented information and application architecture that is difficult to use as a basis for improvement.

Merging quality management and production execution applications into a common process architecture would allow manufacturers to mitigate risk. This can help the business create predictable and compliant product supply in very much the same way that the chemical industry has done in recent years.

Where the healthcare sector is starting is very much based on lessons learned elsewhere, including better organizational integration between the traditionally powerful R&D community of scientists, doctors, and engineers and other elements of the supply network in sourcing, manufacturing, and distribution. The demand-driven strategies being pioneered by the Supply Chain Top 25 cited in Chapter 1 work for both business and the world because the product, supply, and demand domains of the business work together.

Continued business integration

Most large organizations in the industry are the result of mergers and acquisitions from the past decade. Many manufacturers are still consolidating the new organization, rationalizing product and IT portfolios, and integrating applications so that they can cut costs and remove complexity from product supply networks and IT operations. However, even as they settle old acquisitions, new ones are on the horizon. A large number of newer life sciences companies are expected to launch their first drug in the next five years. The high cost of launching a drug or medical device and the synergy and cost savings created by merging mean that these companies are prime targets for takeover by bigger companies. With patents expiring, big pharma is also scrambling to repack its drug pipelines with new products, which is sure to spur a new round of mergers and acquisitions. The recent activity with Boston Scientific and Abbott for Guidant and the bids by Bayer and Merck for Schering are cases in point. Business integration is going to be a continuing issue that affects the global pharmaceutical industry, particularly IT and the organization.

Critical business initiatives: embracing the demand-driven transformation

Turning current business problems into sustained profit and growth opportunities requires that pharmaceutical and life sciences companies adopt demand-driven strategies that target operations excellence and profitable growth and scale. This is going to help companies get their manufacturing houses in order so that they can better serve their business needs and the world.

If pharmaceutical and life sciences organizations are going to meet those needs and address pressing health issues, they need to manufacture products and operate the business with minimum costs and variability, all within regulatory constraints. But pharmaceutical manufacturing is too inefficient as it stands now. Manufacturers are spending proportionally more resources to make products—nearly double in the top 15 pharmaceutical companies—than they are in funding new product development and launch. Six Sigma quality initiatives, lean manufacturing, process control, performance management, and outsourcing projects and methodologies can help in getting this under control and meeting company goals.

Right First Time

Smart companies are cutting operational waste by invoking demand-driven strategies in an effort to make sure the right product is available in the right place at the right time.

These continuous improvement initiatives, underway at such powerhouses as Pfizer, are aimed at improving manufacturing performance and creating predictable product supply. The priorities are to build controllable processes to consistently manufacture products according to validated specifications, ensure specifications are correct and available, and detect product and process defects as they occur, not when products are about to be shipped to market. They also lay the foundation for the FDA's Process Analytical Technology (PAT) Initiative, which uses specialized combinations of technologies to detect and ensure stability at the lowest point of process control based on a scientific understanding of the process.

Establish an active compliance architecture

Progressive companies are also finding ways to turn quality and compliance into an opportunity to improve performance rather than just treating it as a regulatory burden. Quality and compliance must be built into business processes and cultures from the design forward. This means changing traditional metrics and organizational structures (see Chapter 2 for more on organizing for global business). The corporate compliance officer and the regulatory compliance team must move from the more tactical plan of meeting regulatory commitments and firefighting to a proactive role that uses compliance as a competitive advantage. Building compliance into operations and processes will change the culture from quality control silos to quality assurance processes.

Profitable growth and scale

Demand-driven initiatives, customer segmentation and service, and new product launches provide the engine for sustainable growth and revenue enhancement.

Building the demand-driven supply network

Speculation and substitution of products by distributors and wholesalers in downstream processes have forced manufacturers to pay more attention to downstream inventory movements and intelligence.

Unlike their consumer product counterparts that are trying to meet demand and real-time product availability with less inventory and less downstream demand intelligence, life sciences companies are not yet sufficiently integrated through the organization to use demand intelligence to deliver more profitable perfect orders. While the risk of stockouts is a problem in consumer products, it has more dire consequences in life sciences.

Companies like AstraZeneca and Novartis are using produce-to-demand strategies that are based on demand and marry the day-to-day variable demand stream with production, even if only in packaging operations. As a result, produce to demand can be interpreted as *package* to demand to accommodate the differences in product characteristics.

Include strategic contract manufacturing in the business model
Faster product launches and better operational efficiencies can help meet pricing pressures in the industry. The traditional value chain must be transformed into a networked structure that improves operational effectiveness and reduces infrastructure costs throughout the organization. Some companies are turning to contract manufacturers for help. Increasing pressure on once bloated margins has forced big pharmaceutical companies to recognize that they either must excel at in-house manufacturing or farm it out to someone that can do it better. Realizing this, Merck entered into a five-year master supply agreement with contract manufacturer Patheon, in which Patheon will manufacture three of Merck's new products. The same phenomenon is even more advanced in some medical device sectors, where the well-established presence of contract manufacturers that evolved for the consumer electronics industry serves the same purpose.

The challenge with overseas contract manufacturing, however, is that planning horizons lengthen and risks increase. AMR Research surveyed more than 700 companies engaged in contract manufacturing relationships and found that North American or European manufacturers outsourcing to Asia required an additional seven to nine months on the planning horizon. This additional risk demands a more thorough sales and operations planning process—one that allows for the redesign of the supply network to accommodate global contract manufacturing.

Big pharma in Africa: politics, paradoxes, and prescriptions

Swiss pharmaceutical giant Roche is expanding its current activities within sub-Saharan Africa and the world's least developed countries by providing local manufacturers with the technical expertise required to produce generic HIV medicines. Bristol-Myers Squibb has made similar commitments. It's a slow turning of the tide in getting big pharma to address the AIDS epidemic and other diseases in this part of the world. Doing so has been a struggle simply because people cannot afford to pay the high prices of branded drugs, and life sciences companies can't find a way to help while still protecting their interests.

In response, places like Nigeria have seen rampant counterfeiting. The counterfeit drug trade, controlled by the local mafia, is responsible for thousands of deaths every year. And attempts to develop and distribute HIV drugs in South Africa turned into a political and intellectual property fiasco, with court cases involving major global manufacturers. In 2001, the South African government won a three-year battle against 39 large pharmaceutical companies when they objected to legislation passed in 1997 that sought to lower the cost of pharmaceutical drugs. This law made medicines more affordable by allowing parallel imports (buying the cheapest available patented drug), enforcing generic substitution, and implementing price controls. Antiretrovirals for AIDS were a high-profile component of this. When the lawsuit was dropped, activists, trade unionists, and the public at large all hailed it as a massive victory.

The problems of the 4.7 million people infected with AIDS in South Africa, however, did not disappear overnight. Solving the complex issues will take time, effort, and commitment by business, government and nongovernmental organizations, and society itself. If these solutions are going to be sustained, be they healthcare for AIDS or any other needs, businesses must find a way to meet shareholder demands while meeting the needs of the people.

The preventive paradox

Pharmaceutical companies have claimed that R&D and production of low-cost pharmaceuticals is greatly hindered by the lack of IP protection in many countries in Africa. However, the final report of the Commission on Intellectual Property Rights, an initiative of the UK government, asked in its chapter on health, "What role does IP protection play in stimulating R&D on diseases prevalent in developing countries?" This is the answer it uncovered:

"All the evidence we have examined suggests that it hardly plays any role at all, except for those diseases where there is a large market in the developed world (for example, diabetes or heart disease). The heart of the problem is the lack of market demand sufficient to induce the private sector to commit resources to R&D. Therefore, we believe that presence or absence of IP protection in developing countries is of, at best, secondary importance in generating incentives for research directed to diseases prevalent in developing countries."

This is the paradox: the countries that most need certain pharmaceuticals are the countries that can least afford them.

No easy cure

Recognizing that the private sector needs the necessary incentives, the United States and other G8 countries plan to encourage pharmaceutical companies to develop vaccines for diseases that afflict countries too poor to afford them. In February 2006, the G8 nations agreed to a market commitment plan in which they would subsidize the purchase of new vaccines with an incentive package of up to $6 billion. Once the G8 spends the pledged amount, the drug companies would sell the vaccines at a set discount in the developing world. Despite this combination of philanthropy and market mechanisms, the question remains: what workable price guarantees a return just generous enough to get the drug companies involved in a sustainable manner? No answer is complete without also addressing the political environment and posturing associated with these efforts that unfortunately changes by country.

Today, most brand-name pharmaceutical and generic drug companies offer their own discount plans to countries in Africa. At the same time, developing countries can purchase drugs from charities like the Bill and Melinda Gates Foundation and the Clinton Foundation, which have programs that offer low-priced drugs and tests.

Companies like Abbott, Merck, GlaxoSmithKline, and Roche are making significant investments in advanced technologies and manufacturing to meet the growing demand for life-saving drugs in developing countries. Nevertheless, it is hard to say whether such gestures are a public relations move under growing social pressure, or if they will actually lead to tangible results by bringing these drugs at the scale needed for the people that really need them but cannot afford them.

The Clinton Global Initiative

Since leaving office, former President Bill Clinton has made many of the themes in this book part of his post-presidency mission through the Clinton Foundation and its major catalyst, the Clinton Global Initiative, a nonpartisan organization that brings together global leaders to devise and implement innovative solutions to some of the world's most pressing challenges.

In particular, the Clinton Foundation has made the global HIV/AIDS epidemic one of the pillars of its work. While more than 40 million people in the world live with HIV/AIDS, only in the United States and the developed world has it been turned from a death sentence into a manageable disease. In the developing world, with the exception of Brazil, just 700,000 people are receiving antiretroviral treatment, which could mean five to six million people will die of AIDS in the next two years. Such a toll will make it nearly impossible for many countries in the developing world to "achieve their social and economic development goals, and the future of our global community will be at risk," the foundation explains.

Planning for the future

The pharmaceutical and life sciences landscape is changing rapidly. In the future, companies won't be able to count on blockbuster drugs to provide double-digit growth and a substantial portion of revenue. The prohibitive costs to develop new drugs means fewer reach the development stage and even fewer reach the market. To compete, organizations must make regulatory compliance integral to operations, build a demand-driven operation, and change their organizations to meet the new demands. Doing so will result in savings of hundreds of millions of dollars, faster new product development, and a better chance at success in an increasingly competitive market. With threats like a pandemic from the avian flu, a healthy healthcare industry is more important than ever.

Pandemic: Readiness Is Low and Risk Is High

The H5N1 avian flu virus has evolved into two genetically distinct strains that some U.S. scientists fear increases the risk to humans. While the question about whether it will mutate into a human-transmissible form still lingers, U.S. officials warn that it's now a matter of when—not if—the virus will land on North American shores.

In a December 2005 report, the Congressional Budget Office prepared an assessment of possible macroeconomic effects of an avian flu pandemic and modeled two scenarios in the United States. In the first scenario—the severe one—roughly 90 million people become sick and 2 million people die, with the GDP taking a hit of 5 percent in the subsequent year.

In the second scenario, the mild one, about 75 million people are infected and 100,000 die, with the GDP taking a hit of one and a half percent. Companies need to face reality that such a pandemic, when it comes, will kill on a large scale. Morbidity rates are currently greater than 50 percent among humans who have contracted the H5N1 flu strain (see Figure 2). This is a massive global risk scenario not just on human life, but on the economic health of every country in the world. Companies should be actively working on risk management strategies, from managing supply and logistics risk to preparing for business continuity and supply chain resilience in the face of any unexpected event.

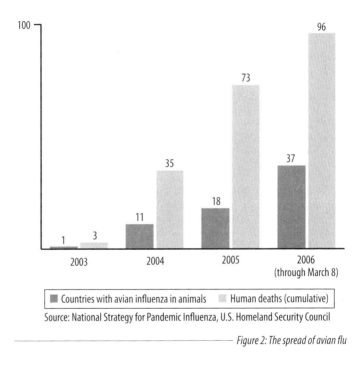

Source: National Strategy for Pandemic Influenza, U.S. Homeland Security Council

Figure 2: The spread of avian flu

Are you ready?

To assess how companies are preparing for a major business disruption and its ramifications, AMR Research surveyed companies about their level of readiness for an avian flu pandemic. Overall, 32% say they are ready. Here's a more detailed look at the readiness of their contingency plans:

- Risk management—43%
- Homebound—38%
- Self-service—29%
- Training—22%
- Supply risk—22%

So while 43 percent of firms say they have a policy in place for assessing their risk in the event of a catastrophic event like a pandemic, nearly 60 percent don't. For many, though, plans are in the evaluation stage. Even more telling is that firms are abysmally unprepared for risk to supply. This is backed by other AMR Research survey results on supply chain risk management that show supply reliability and managing supply risk are top areas of concern (see Figure 3). In short, companies are aware of and worried about risk, but still aren't prepared for it.

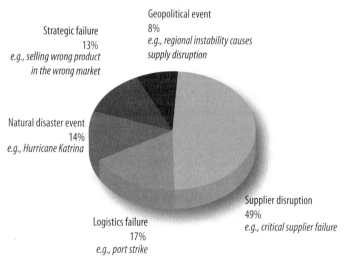

Figure 3: What area of supply chain risk most keeps you awake at night?

131

While some industries are more prepared than others, the general state of readiness for an event like a pandemic is low. Those industries that reported high readiness are many of the ones that will be on the front lines of a pandemic, such as the transportation sector. However, at the other end of the spectrum, retail, industrial manufacturing, and energy companies are very low on the readiness scale. Data on pharmaceutical firms—another critical link—is mixed. The small survey sample of pharmaceutical respondents reported above-average levels of readiness, but interviews with pharmaceutical firms reveals more of a mixed bag. Some with established risk management practices, like Haemonetics and Eli Lilly, were able to integrate pandemic planning smoothly into their risk management framework. However, other prominent pharmaceutical firms report they either have no plans or there is no communication of those plans.

Predicting the pandemic: what pharmaceutical manufacturers should be thinking

Pharmaceutical companies must plan at a much more detailed level than anything undertaken thus far if they are to tackle the potential catastrophe of a pandemic head on. They must be able to deal with the human and economic consequences to the supply chain and the rest of the organization. Companies must develop intensive scenario planning using simulation tools and model their manufacturing along with their global supply chains to be able to react to the scenarios. The likely effect of catastrophic events to the business and IT environment needs to be evaluated, and action plans with clear command-and-control components must be put in place. Detail planning structures, tools, and accountabilities need to be allocated as soon as possible.

FDA hurdles

Flu vaccines are currently produced through time-consuming, antiquated processes that use chicken eggs as hosts. More than 70 percent of global supply is produced in this manner by CSL, Glaxo-SmithKline (and its ID Biomedical subsidiary), Chiron, and Sanofi

Pasteur. Even with expanding capacities, pharmaceutical production facilities are unlikely to meet global demand for conventional vaccines in time to avert a pandemic.

However, promising new technologies to mass-produce vaccines, such as cell-based or DNA-based methods, are being successfully tested in animals. Baxter and Solvay Pharmaceuticals are investing heavily in new vaccine manufacturing methods. With such techniques, a matched vaccine can potentially be mass produced within four weeks instead of the three to six months when using currently available and FDA-approved methods. Venture capital (VC) firms have also started backing the development of new technologies to combat pandemics. Kleiner Perkins Caufield & Byers, Silicon Valley's premier VC firm, has launched a $200 million fund to invest in companies developing drugs, disease detection techniques, and other products aimed at fighting global pandemics. This fund will concentrate on smaller companies like BioCryst Pharmaceuticals, which are developing new ways to get drugs to market faster.

New technologies have not been tested on humans, however, and it could be years before they are commercialized. The FDA, working closely with the Centers for Disease Control (CDC), must collaborate with researchers and pharmaceutical manufacturers to speed the development, manufacture, and deployment of vaccines using new technologies. Although the FDA is comfortable using new technologies for pandemic influenza vaccines, it will require more convincing before allowing manufacturers to produce cell-culture-based vaccines for conventional flu strains. As a result, manufacturers will be hesitant to invest in capacity dedicated to just one influenza strain, with the cost of building a new facility ranging from $50 million to $400 million.

If the crisis hits, the FDA must also take a hard look at antitrust and patent laws to make sure that it is not impeding the path of companies looking to collaborate to produce life-saving drugs. The FDA must take the lead in tearing down existing legal and cultural walls, thus creating a community of cooperation and interaction between key players that will be involved in beating the pandemic.

Opportunistic demand: lessons from retail

Life sciences companies need to gauge demand, whether it be for protective clothing and masks or medicines and vaccines. They must ensure that they have their products at the right place at the right time so as not to face stockouts, much like The Home Depot and Wal-Mart in the retail sector have done with supplies in times of natural disaster. This is the right time to demonstrate leadership in the community and benefit from the goodwill. They must also make the best use of their production capacity and design a supply chain based on agility, inventory strategies, and perceived supply risk (see Chapter 6 for more on supply agility).

The time is now

For all companies, regardless of industry, supply chain risk management is not just about conducting a business continuity audit, building a continuity plan, and sticking it in a binder on some executive's shelf. It's about putting in place a program to assess the risks that supply chains may face and building a plan for mitigating those risks. In the area of an unexpected event like a pandemic, firms are unprepared to manage the risk of supplier disruption, training and cross-training employees, and supporting customers and suppliers remotely. Ignoring the possibility of a pandemic or other low-probability, high-impact events is not a strategy—building a risk management framework is.

If firms have not developed supply chain risk management practices yet, they must—and quickly. Today's supply chains are global, running lean and highly interconnected. Failure at one node in the supply chain, whether it's a supplier in China or the corner grocery store, can leave a company highly exposed. Said differently, in event of failure, a supply chain is only as strong as its weakest link. Well-prepared supply networks will survive and thrive in the event of a pandemic or other major event. To be prepared, companies should consider doing the following:

· **Document** the potential risks that face your supply chain and focus on the most likely, highest-impact event and the product lines that matter the most to profitability or margin of the suppliers that create the most volume.

- **Assess** the supplier and logistics networks for risk, likelihood of supplier failure, and other risks. Develop mitigation plans for the highest-risk suppliers, lanes, and commodities.
- **Implement** an ongoing risk management process and plan so that as new sources of supply are added, new products are introduced, new projects are initiated, and the portfolio fits within the risk tolerance of the risk management process.

Remember that no strategy is not a strategy. Supply chain risk management will reduce risks for your enterprise, eliminate potential and unexpected costs, reduce disruptions, improve overall supply chain performance, and produce competitive advantage for the companies that do it right.

Prepping for pandemic: top five actions to take now

What follows are technology investments that can yield relatively quick wins to prepare for a pandemic. As such, we focus on niche applications and service providers that provide immediate functionality and service as opposed to long enterprise deployments.

Supply risk planning

Designing the flexible supply network means that the organization has alternative nodes that can act as suppliers or logisticians should the primary node fail because of a pandemic in the region or other factors. Working in simulation, the organization can determine the effect of such changes, answering the key question: what is the change in lead time, cost, quality, and reliability? With a series of simulated what-ifs, the prepared organization can have alternative suppliers ready.

Results of this investment in a pandemic
The risk of switching to alternative sources has been examined. Prenegotiated agreements can potentially block out competitors from using this source.

Results of this investment without a pandemic
Having an alternative source can provide negotiating power as well as mitigate risks of smaller disasters and local disruptions.

Homebound

As people stay at home, more business will be conducted by phone and the Internet. Increased capacity and functionality will be needed to handle complaints, manage cases, access help desks and product information, and dispatch service personnel. Traditionally, this functionality is deployed for retail-oriented businesses. However, suppliers and employees will need to access information as traditional points of contact may not be available. Telephony hardware will be needed to support erratic spikes in volume, and companies will need to support a flexible workforce that includes home workers.

Results of this investment in a pandemic

Business can continue, keeping the economy afloat and allowing companies to meet the needs of the public.

Results of this investment without a pandemic

Better customer service, decreased cost of sale, and redundant operations in preparation for future economic, social, or natural disasters are all benefits.

Self-service

Some companies may choose to accelerate ongoing efforts that let their customers, employees, and other constituents conduct business electronically. This can be in the form of employees updating HR records, customers ordering product, or suppliers accessing payment information. A system designed to minimize human intervention in fulfilling an order will help sustain ongoing operations with limited staff. Along with niche vendors, service providers will benefit from such projects. Existing enterprise resource planning (ERP) systems will provide some required functionality, but new process designs that can support the self-service model and still ensure all corporate policies and procedures are met will have to be implemented.

Results of this investment in a pandemic
Business continues with limited in-house staff.

Results of this investment without a pandemic
The cost of labor in fulfilling routine orders is reduced.

Training

Whether it's information for a specific sales account, understanding a manufacturing machine's particular quirks, or getting payroll information, when the ability to perform simple functions disappears, a company is paralyzed. Short-term benefits come from getting employees to use already-deployed applications. Companies often have adequate functionality, but employees cannot or simply refuse to use it. Services and training may yield quick results. Longer term investments that build on collaboration, content management, portals, and search will yield strong knowledge management. Companies can also invest in human capital management applications. Two specific niches, skills management and contingent worker management applications, allow companies to take immediate action to fill voids.

Results of this investment in a pandemic
Companies can continue to function as a viable business with little disruption as replacements are found for employees and groups that are not available to work.

Results of this investment without a pandemic
Collaboration between employees spurs innovation and helps companies beat competitors to market. It reduces the chance of making the same mistake twice, and mitigates the inevitable loss of knowledge because of an aging or migrant workforce. Also, skills-based succession plans will decrease the effects of losing key workers.

Risk management

Many companies already have some form of risk management in place after investing in tools for compliance, analytics, and business intelligence for process management. Companies need to apply the same processes used to evaluate investments (payback/return on investment) to evaluate the risk of rectifying a potential problem because of a pandemic. For instance, cash will become an issue in a disjointed world. Customers may be booking their own orders, but companies must consider cash flow. Are customers' payables departments at full staff? Are they paying bills on time? These scenarios should become part of the modeled cash flow projections.

Results of this investment in a pandemic

Operations continue because of informed choices, strong cash management, and appropriate proactive investment.

Results of this investment without a pandemic

The company can make informed choices for all investments.

Risk Management:
The Supply Chain Responds | 5

Risk Management: The Supply Chain Responds

Globalization has brought new energy and opportunity to businesses around the world, but in the process has exposed operations to a dramatically wider ripple effect whenever trouble hits. Risk management, traditionally the province of finance, has lately become an essential discipline for supply chain professionals tasked to source and deliver globally while limiting exposure to disaster. The discipline naturally extends to helping communities and people in distress, as seen in New Orleans after Hurricane Katrina.

Much business risk is outside a company's control, whether it's a hurricane, a supplier that fails without warning, energy costs that double in a matter of weeks, or, as seen in Chapter 4, health crises in the form of a global pandemic. Supply chain risk management means planning for threats, having contingency plans to keep business going, and using intelligent risk hedging to cap exposure.

In Chapter 5, we define the concepts of risk management and map the strategies companies can put into place to help moderate the unpredictable world. The chapter also provides case studies of companies that have found ways to mitigate risk and, in some cases, directly improve the bottom line with these strategies. Finally, we include some of the strategies governments and businesses are pulling together to help secure both supply and people in this increasingly interdependent global economy.

Risk and the Supply Chain

PART
ONE

The supply chain organization is constantly involved in placing informed bets that involve calculated risks. The questions it is asking: "Can we beat a competitor to market with our new product? Will suppliers be able to ramp up volume since our forecast was too low? How can we source this new custom part to meet our quality, performance, and reliability requirements? How should we prepare for disaster?"

Business—global, local, green, or demand driven—always involves risk. And virtually all business decisions involve a degree of uncertainty, whether it's about the success of a product launch, conditions of the economy, or the ability of the supply base to deliver what was promised, when it was promised, and at the level of quality expected.

Basic risk management theory holds that a company or an investor must take on more risk in order to attain a return on investment that exceeds the general market or industry rate of return. Companies routinely make high-risk, high-reward bets on future products—look to the pharmaceutical or consumer electronics industries for numerous examples—but balance those risks across a portfolio of products. Rarely does a firm bet it all on one product and live to tell about it.

Defining risk

Risk management is the process of measuring or assessing risk and then developing strategies to manage the risk. Supply chain risk management strategies can involve the transference of risk to another party, risk avoidance or mitigation, or channel risk sharing.

The following are balanced by supply chain management risk assessments:

· Probability of demand
· Likelihood of reliable supply
· Most effective allocation of resources
· Probability of success of new product introductions
· Market conditions
· Opportunity costs of alternative decision paths

The practice of supply chain risk management is growing in importance as a discipline because supply chains are running leaner and more efficiently, and are becoming more demand driven. At the same time, demand has become more variable, and product configuration, customization, and customer service expectations have skyrocketed. Meanwhile, supply networks have grown global, introducing longer, more variable lead times and increasing the possible risks that brand owners must manage.

A major A&D company had a problem. It was averaging two significant supplier failures per year and had no proactive supplier risk management process. The company faced costs of $10 million or more a year, with no systematic way to reduce the risk in its supply base of 11,000 suppliers.

The failures

- *In one case, the firm had become so reliant on a specific supplier, funneling $800 million in orders its way, that when significant financial and manufacturing quality problems surfaced and business failure was imminent, it had no choice but to take over the company. It also had to relocate several critical resources on site to run the operations. Cost: an estimated $5 million.*
- *A foreign-owned substrate supplier ceased operations one day with no warning. Workers arrived at the factory and found the gates locked. The absence of the component, which was vital material for several solid-state devices, disrupted a number of ongoing projects. Cost: another estimated $5 million.*

In 2005 alone, the A&D firm had submitted 5,300 project proposals (approximately 17 per day) and had been awarded 3,200 contracts (about 10 per day). The reliability and quality of supply are critical to profitably deliver on these commitments.

The fix

The company redesigned its process, moving risk management responsibility out of the ivory tower of finance and distributing it among the real owners—the buyer community for supplier selection and supply risk management, and program managers to rally the need for proactive risk management.

The firm took two steps to shore up its supply risk management process:
- *Consolidated the supplier masters and proactively linked in third-party data on the supply base. This step required rigor, mapping several tiers into the supply base to make sure risk managers understood parent-child relationships and the risk relationships between Tier 1 suppliers and their parents and siblings.*
- *Purchased and implemented an online system that works as an early warning system to flag supplier risks before they become problems based on pattern recognition of early warning indicators.*

The results

15 new suppliers have been blocked for being high risk, avoiding potential un-anticipated cost and/or supply disruption, in the year since its implementation (and not all suppliers are online yet). Some 300 orders across 100 suppliers were stopped and redirected to new suppliers. As an ancillary benefit, intimacy and knowledge of the supply base are greatly enhanced, and no new $5 million sup-plier blowups have occurred.

By its own admission, the firm recognizes that risk management benefits can be difficult to measure. The leader of this program compares it to the value of insurance. Was your policy worth owning even if you did not have to use it?

In his book, *Fooled by Randomness: The Hidden Role of Chance in the Markets and in Life*, Nassim Nicholas Taleb makes the convincing argument that chance, luck, and variability—or randomness—play a larger role in life, markets, and supply chains than they get credit for. Models often underestimate real variability and rely too heav-ily on analytical oversimplifications like normal distributions. Noise is attributed meaning, and many overreact to data that is in fact noise, but outliers in data that may contain important infor-mation are ignored. On top of that, human beings do not naturally think probabilistically. The process of risk management, however, requires understanding the probability of the occurrence of un-likely but high-impact events, such as critical supplier failure, port strike, natural disaster, or energy price spike, and the appropriate means to manage and mitigate those risks.

Demand-driven supply networks require supply chain risk management practices

The idea of supply chain risk management as a practice is gain-ing currency. Early data from a field study tendered by AMR Re-search shows approximately 30 percent of firms currently employ supply chain risk management techniques and systems, while 50 percent are implementing or planning to evaluate supply chain risk management technology in the next year or two. (Part Two of this chapter outlines strategies for addressing risk).

The study also finds 36 percent have dedicated specific funding to supply chain risk management, with the remainder coming from general operations, IT, or finance budgets. Additionally, 56 percent of firms are increasing their spending on supply chain risk management in 2006. Other AMR Research surveys show supplier failure as the top concern among supply chain practitioners, followed by strategic risk, such as selling the wrong product at the wrong time in the wrong market, and logistics risk. Firms are struggling to get a handle on understanding the risks and interdependencies in their supply chains and developing strategies to allay those risks.

Best practices

Forecast and plan for risk and uncertainty

Sound like an oxymoron? Despite the unpredictability of disruptions, techniques can be employed to better prepare for and diminish the effect of certain supply chain risks. As one planner for a Florida-based grocery chain said, "Planning for the hurricane season requires a combination of lessons from past experiences, expectations for the coming season, and leveraging what we know—our tribal knowledge." The grocer prebuilds inventory for vital items, such as diapers, bottled water, and batteries (as well as for unexpected items learned from past seasons, like Pop-Tarts), a month before the start of hurricane season. The team then has a complete action plan for when and what to order when a hurricane strikes, and how to spread delivery risk across second and third sources of supply. Instead of workers scrambling to plan, they are scrambling to get the stores operating, with orders sent to suppliers before the larger competitors.

Planners use sophisticated probabilistic forecasting techniques to assess the risk of running out of stock in the event of promotions or other factors. They use inventory optimization techniques to spread risk across nodes and minimize the impact of unexpected events, putting themselves in position to respond quicker to sudden changes in supply or demand.

Develop a method for assessing current risk

Prepared companies meticulously map out their supply bases, taking careful note of parent-child relationships between suppliers, balance-of-trade relationships, and the logistics network used by their suppliers. They develop and monitor indicators of supplier performance to generate a multidimensional scorecard approach that lets them assess whether risk is rising or falling.

A biotechnology company developed seven criteria against which each and every supplier was scored, helping the firm identify high-risk suppliers that needed more management. An A&D company applied a similar technique, using predictive analytics on financial, quality, and other performance indicators to try to predict failures before they happen.

Organize for risk

Companies are also adjusting to make supply risk management work as an ongoing competency rather than an annual exercise that ends up in a binder on a bookshelf. These companies emphasize the importance of a cross-functional team that usually involves supply chain, finance, and operations reporting to an executive steering committee, but often involves quality, safety, and engineering personnel as well. Care must also be given to the implementation of the process.

Firms have to make a conscious choice between centralizing and decentralizing risk management responsibility by either empowering individuals across the organization within a framework of standards or centralizing the process to ensure compliance at the expense of more active, field-level supplier management.

Risk Management Strategies

Supply chain risk management strategies allow demand-driven companies to reduce the effects of demand variability and lower their supply risks. To have a feasible plan, it is no longer acceptable to just match demand with supply. You must analyze demand signals and plan performance and the supply base for agility and risk mitigation.

Risk management is all old hat for financial managers. Many of the techniques used in financial management can be applied to supply chains as well, particularly as they become more global and complex. However, while financial risk management deals with factors that can be managed through traded financial instruments, supply chain risk management is broader. Supply chain risk assessments balance the probability of demand, likelihood of reliable supply, most effective allocation of resources, probability of successful new product introductions, market conditions, and opportunity costs of alternative decision paths.

Don't confuse supply chain risk management with agility (see Chapter 6). While supply chain agility is defined as moving quickly and with ease, supply chain risk balances business risks against the opportunity cost of no decision. Agility and risk mitigation are complementary strategies, but not interchangeable.

With this in mind, here are some strategies to help get a handle on risk. The factors are organized into 10 strategies and applied to the demand-driven supply network model (see Figure 1). They are divided between managing demand, supply, and product as well as the overlapping areas between the three.

Managing demand risks

Strategy No. 1: customer rationalization

All customers are not equal. In fact, many customer commitments threaten profitability. Ever had a sales representative promise a 99 percent service level and sign a service-level agreement when the supply chain lacks reliable supply? This is risk in the making. Sometimes the right answer is to limit the product line or walk away. Consider the case of one company that launches 30 new SKUs per month. With 1,400 active items, the company found that 8 out of 10 customers buy only 125 products. Of those products, 20 represent 80 percent of the volume. Through customer and product rationalization, the marketing and finance team returned $350 million in incremental sales in 2004. Sales forces that are not equally rewarded on revenue and profitability will continually expose a company to risk.

Strategy No. 2: price management and risk sharing

The first principle of economics is market pricing. However, only a few demand-driven leaders incorporate price management analysis into category management, forecasting, and sales and operations planning (S&OP). For many in price-sensitive markets, this is an opportunity. Actively investigate price management sensitivity analysis as a means of reducing risk in demand-management and demand-shaping activities.

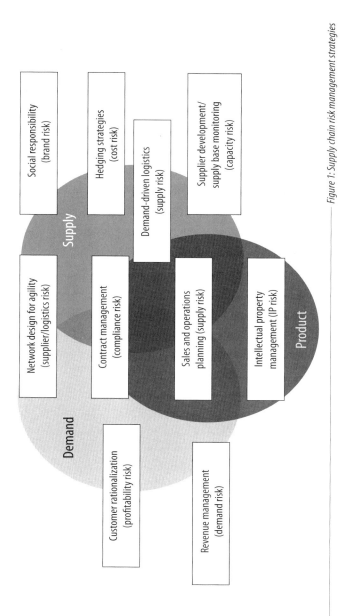

Figure 1: Supply chain risk management strategies

Managing supply risks

Strategy No. 3: social responsibility for brand owners
The most important asset of the company is the brand. Supply strategies and relationship management with suppliers can help prevent the brand from tarnishing and even improve the brand's perception. Look at the turnaround of brand perception of Wal-Mart in the United States. Social responsibility positioning and supplier management are used to strengthen growing brands like Starbucks and Whole Foods (see Chapter 3 for more on social responsibility and profitability). Social responsibility in sourcing is growing in importance for brand owners as a risk mitigation strategy. Companies should have clear strategies, using them as a parameter in supplier rationalization programs and supply-based modeling and as a factor in multivariate bidding with e-sourcing tools.

In the aftermath of Katrina

Many of the basic assumptions of a supply chain—the availability of supply, lead times, demand, and logistics—changed when Hurricane Katrina hit the Gulf Coast. Here are five ways businesses can shore up their supply chains in the wake of future disasters.

1. Rerun demand plans
Katrina moved the point of purchase for about 11 percent of the volume of most companies. Retail stores and distributors were closed, with products being purchased at other locations and then routed into the affected areas. The demand for products also changed. The market shifted to lumber, nails—the basics—and remains so. It's no longer a market for fashion or luxury goods, and won't be for some time. When disaster hits, companies need to work with customer service and logistics teams to remap volume, rethink market demand, and rerun demand plans immediately to translate independent to dependent demand for suppliers.

2. Strategize cross-functionally on guaranteeing supply for key customers
Critical products are in short supply in a disaster. As customer service teams work to allocate these products to affected areas, agreement and visibility of customer, channel, and product priorities are critical. Develop clear definitions and understanding for all customer, service, and logistics teams to ensure the right products get to the right customers in time.

3. Rethink logistics
Prepare for logistics problems. The Gulf Coast was fraught with logistic difficulties as ocean, barge, and land freight were all compromised by the hurricane. The five major ports in the Mississippi River basin that halted operations—South Louisiana, New Orleans, Baton Rouge, Plaquemines, and Mobile—move an annual volume of 450 million tons of cargo, more than six and a half times the volume of Long Beach and three times the ports in New York and New Jersey. Companies must have network design technologies in place to reroute when disaster strikes and streamline operations.

4. Focus on relationships to ensure reliable supply
Price escalation and the tightening of critical supplies are a reality. In the wake of Katrina, sugar cane lay in the fields, and many cotton crops were flattened. Oil, chemicals, and seafood were all affected. The area is also a major artery of critical imports, such as bananas, rubber, metals, and coffee. The winning strategies were those that focused on reliable supply. Relationships and collaboration were key. Many buy-side contracts will need to be renegotiated to reflect the business climate in such cases. Head-to-head confrontation with suppliers to enforce a buy-side contract will result in unpredictable supply.

5. Marshal supplies to help
Many items that were in critical need in the Southeast were available in many supply chains as excess and obsolete inventories. Food, water, clothing, shoes, diapers, and pharmaceuticals were badly needed. It was a time for companies to marshal their supply chains to help the cause and work closely with the established relief agencies to coordinate supplies to the area.

Strategy No. 4: hedging strategies to mitigate cost risks

Spikes in prices for energy, copper, metals, sugar, and other core raw materials make companies more aware of risks caused by rising raw material costs. Virtually all companies have some experience with hedging, often with currency to manage fluctuations (although outside of the airline and automotive industries, along with cutting-edge companies within selected other industries, hedging strategies are in their infancy). Some raw-material-sensitive companies maintain a trading desk that is managed as a profit center, taking long or short positions in materials based on their analysis of the market. In leading companies, however, procurement and supply chain organizations partner together to consider the demand forecast, competition for supply, and market conditions to use hedging strategies to better compete through reduced costs and assurance of supply.

Southwest flies high with hedging

In an industry where fuel prices are cutting deep into profits, Southwest Airlines is soaring. With reported earnings of $174 million (excluding unrealized gains from hedging activities), it delivered 46 percent year-over-year profit growth for 3Q05—its 58th consecutive profitable quarter. Most notable was the $295 million Southwest saved from fuel hedging contracts; the savings generated from its hedging program equated to 1.7 times its reported profit of $174 million. Without the hedging gains, Southwest would have reported a sizable quarterly loss, not unlike many of its competitors.

At Southwest, procurement and sourcing is an executive priority. Its use of hedging is part of a demand-driven commodity strategy with a long-term planning horizon. With the program, planned through 2009, Southwest reduces the volatility of its cost structure and gives the company the financial security to compete aggressively in a tough market.

Being demand driven is vital to procurement and the effective deployment of hedging strategies. To achieve this level of visibility for future requirements planning, companies must inject procurement organizations and strategy into S&OP processes, and extend the forecast duration to support the commodity strategy planning period.

154

Strategy No. 5: demand-driven logistics to mitigate supply risk

Global supply chains are now the standard, not the exception. Nonetheless, port backups in Long Beach during Christmas 2004 highlighted one of the risks of extended supply chains and the uncertainties amplified by longer lead times, port congestion, near-capacity transportation networks, and customer issues.

It's not just ports, though. Truck driver shortages and new regulations, like the Working Time Directive in the UK that limits the workload of drivers, are also reaping havoc on transportation. A chief of operations at a $25 billion global company says his No. 1 worry is the conditions of roads and deteriorating logistics infrastructure in the United States. It's going to get worse as manufacturing increasingly moves to places like China, with logistics (and supply visibility) becoming life or death processes in a demand-driven world (see Table 1).

	2002–2003	2003–2004
Not realizing magnitude	You think: China doesn't matter	
	56%	33%
	You think: China as supplier	
	18%	19%

	U.S.-China imports	
Soaring growth in China trade	$125B	$156B (+29%)
	U.S.-China exports	
	$22B	$28B (+22%)

	U.S. truckload demand versus supply index*	
Inadequate infrastructure	4.5:1	10:1

* Oct. 2004 Morgan Stanley (dry van only) demand versus supply index

Table 1: China—are we ready?

But there is hope. Transportation management and visibility systems increasingly model global networks and can help companies respond to unexpected changes in the network. In concert, inventory management in the form of inventory policies, postponement strategies, and inventory buffers can help manage the risks of supply and delivery uncertainty.

Strategy No. 6: supplier development for reliable supply

Managing supply risks starts with the supply base. Is a supplier creditworthy? Do you have visibility to manufacturing capacity? Do suppliers have good on-time delivery performance and high product quality? Do suppliers comply with your corporate statements on social responsibility and fair labor rules? Risks associated with suppliers include unexpected breaking of commitments that strand companies with no inventory, unexpected supplier bankruptcy (which is hard to monitor for offshore suppliers), and huge brand liabilities if suppliers do not match social responsibility criteria. Active supplier scorecarding and monitoring can provide an early warning system to raise visibility to problems. Audits are proving largely ineffective, but technology is evolving to support supply base monitoring.

Managing product risks

Strategy No. 7: IP management risk mitigation

As companies think through the risk of design pirating, they are designing their supply chains to protect intellectual property (IP). One shoe manufacturer has the tops of its sneakers sewn in Asia and the soles manufactured in Mexico. It saves the manufacture of its special heel gels (the company's competitive advantage) for production in the United States, with final assembly by a third-party logistics firm. This network is designed to protect IP and improve responsiveness. Supply networks must be designed to protect product design information, an increasingly important factor in the definition of global networks (see Chapter 2 for more on protecting IP in China).

The overlap between supply, demand, and product management

Strategy No. 8: network design for agility

The use of network design and optimization tools should be a top priority for companies seeking to minimize risk. With the movement to longer supply chains with Asian outsourcing and the focus on new product introductions, demand-driven companies are rethinking their networks yearly and fine-tuning them quarterly. The range has also broadened. Today it is not uncommon to see the modeling of the competition, tax and currency fluctuations, new product introduction launches, supplier rationalization strategies, and product mix optimization.

China revaluation and supply chain risk

China's currency being allowed to float freely to its fair market exchange rate is a risk that must be watched. The issue for manufacturers pushing large amounts of their supply base deeper into China's low-cost economy is that a big chunk of the cost advantage has been artificial because of the yuan being pegged to the dollar. Business risk was heightened by the political nature of exchange rate determination—something inherently unpredictable as politics works in its own mysterious ways, often indifferent to the needs of business.

Now that revaluation is a reality, the real lesson is just how smart and business-friendly this political process is proving to be. The adjustments Beijing has made have been widely applauded as an appropriate symbolic move, but a big way from closing the 40 percent gap in exchange rates that some experts believe is ultimately warranted. Policy makers can take comfort that trade imbalances are recognized and will be getting attention from Beijing. Business customers with big supply chain bets in China can take comfort that political pressure will not be allowed to build until it bursts, and that cherished cost advantages will be protected as long as possible.

China has demonstrated its intent to manage political risk with an eye to its business goals—one less thing for sourcing and manufacturing managers in the United States and Europe to worry about in their supply chain strategies.

Strategy No. 9: buy-side contract management to improve compliance

In third-generation sourcing and procurement applications, buy-side contract management plays an increasingly important role. The bridge between sourcing and procurement links legal, procurement, and financial departments together to view and manage risk. Use contract management techniques first for visibility into your commitments and potential liabilities, and then use contracts as assets, building in flexibility to reduce risk exposure.

Strategy No. 10: S&OP for a realistic and profitable supply plan

Demand-driven companies are aggressively modeling and determining the right level of risk in their S&OP scenarios. Scenario planning is being redefined to manage risk of demand and against supply reliability. S&OP continues to be at the core of demand-driven leadership strategies. The twist is the movement of scenario planning not only to consider supply, demand, and profitability, but also evaluate the scenarios for agility and risk.

Security is vital, but at what price?

Everyone wants to be confident that growing international supply chains are secure and homeland security (or global security, for that matter) isn't threatened. The trick is to figure out how to do this without inhibiting the delicate balance of the global economy. Some national security officials report the likelihood of an attack through the global supply chain is so high that it is a matter of when, not if. How can countries establish secure supply chains without slowing the flow of the economy or imposing overly restrictive costs? One solution is using more information, process automation, and new technologies not just by U.S. corporations, shipping companies, and domestic ports, but also at factories and facilities with international origins.

The government currently has a two-part approach: corporate voluntary participation in a cooperative program called Customs-Trade Partnership Against Terrorism (C-TPAT), and requiring trading partners to transmit information that the government can collect and analyze in its new trade processing system, the Automated Commercial Environment (ACE).

C-TPAT

C-TPAT requires corporations assume responsibility for the security of their supply chains well in advance of the normal legal responsibility (when the company takes possession of the goods). Customs asks companies to ensure and monitor security practices and execution from the origin, through transit, to the ports, and delivery to final destination. The higher a company progresses in C-TPAT status, the more benefits it can receive, mostly in the form of expedited flow of shipments through customs. But smart companies would add the marketing value into this equation as consumers become more savvy about security issues, much like they have with fair labor standards and green manufacturing. As of 2005, C-TPAT members accounted for 42 percent of all imports by volume.

The cooperative program has three tiers:

- **Tier 1**—A company attests that it has performed a risk analysis of its supply chain and has taken steps to mitigate any vulnerabilities. Approximately 5,800 companies have been accepted by customs.
- **Tier 2**—Requires that the attestation be validated by customs officials. Almost 3,800 corporations have either achieved this status or are in the process of being validated.
- **Tier 3**—These companies must continuously follow supply chain security best practices, although customs hasn't declared an official definition of what that is. Approximately 130 companies have reached this level to date.

ACE

For its own efforts, customs is banking on its trade processing system, ACE, due by 2010. Under ACE, importers must send increasingly detailed information to customs prior to arrival at a border crossing. Those that don't will find significant delays. Those that do it well will eventually be in the fast lane when crossing customs.

Companies should prepare for flexible and adaptable information flows, possibly integrated from multiple systems, to support what will most likely be an increasing information requirement. In fact, customs is piloting a new program it calls the Advanced Trade Data Initiative (ATDI), which will require much more information about shipments, travel paths, and so forth. The difficulty with ATDI will be getting all the parties in the supply chain network to provide the right information with quality, accuracy, and timeliness—the same things, oddly enough, that the industry struggles with today in attempting supply chain collaboration.

The time to act is now

Early pioneers are reporting significantly reduced container inspections. One consumer goods company says it slashed imported container inspections to a mere 0.66 percent from 7.60 percent. This faster flow of goods can shrink overall inventory buffers, and supply chain transparency can be used to help control unexpected lead-time variability: turning requirements into profits. Companies should be developing strategies now for supporting higher levels of transparency across their entire supply chain network, building flexible systems to share more information, and adopting practices for evaluating the security practices of their partners.

The Practitioner's Guide | 6

The Practitioner's Guide

Whether your goal is saving the world or just getting promoted, life for supply chain professionals today is far more complex than 20 years ago, when clear departmental lines meant basic tasks with minimal uncertainty. Globalization, the rising importance of risk management, and new social challenges like environmental sustainability, third-world development, and crushing healthcare costs combine to elevate the importance of supply chain as a career.

Responding to business pressures that demand greater operational agility means understanding the strategic implications of tradeoffs being made every day. Rising to the occasion as world problems find their way onto supply chain executives' agendas calls for very much the same skills. Tools of the trade are essential to handle these challenges as businesses seek to develop demand-driven supply networks.

Chapter 6 is a summary of some practical tools that AMR Research has developed or uncovered in our field research and work with clients over the past two decades. First, five essential strategies for becoming demand driven are explained with examples. Second, the vital concept of supply chain agility is defined and applied. Finally, our supply chain benchmarking toolset is detailed with definitions of critical performance metrics and enablers.

Becoming Demand Driven

PART
ONE

Implementing a socially responsible yet profitable supply chain while operating in a global economy and being agile enough to navigate risks demands being...well, demand driven.

Those companies that lead in demand-driven supply network (DDSN) efforts do more *demand sensing*, have more efforts for *demand shaping*, and aim for a profitable *demand response*. AMR Research benchmarking data shows the most advanced demand-sensing companies enjoy huge benefits:

- 10 percent more revenue
- 5 to 7 percent better profit margins
- 15 percent less inventory
- 17 percent better perfect order performance
- 35 percent shorter cash-to-cash cycle time

Five essential strategies for becoming demand driven

Those seeing these types of results are using cross-functional, coordinated efforts for demand-sensing strategies, demand-shaping processes, and a corporate understanding of how to achieve a profitable demand response. While these efforts vary by line of business, they can be distilled into five strategies.

Strategy No. 1: Market driven, not marketing driven

Demand-driven companies understand their customers and markets. In these companies, processes are built from the outside-in, based on a clear view of the customer, what is important to the customer, and the requirements for account profitability. These companies become zealots for a new product introductions and using their supply networks to shape and respond to demand.

Marketing and sales organizations must own the corporate forecast, lead corporate efforts for demand-sensing and demand-shaping activities, and create cross-functional support teams to quickly respond to demand.

Customer data powers the supply chain, yet less than one percent of companies use customer data as the basis for supply chain planning processes, and less than two percent segment customers based on profitability. One global supplier of consumer electronics recognized this as a huge problem. With an internal sales forecast running at a 55 percent error rate, it knew there had to be a better way.

With no single customer representing more than 20 percent of volume, and with big-box retailers representing 85 percent of the total volume, this company's management decided to build a collaborative sales and operations planning (S&OP) process with its retail partners. As it began its efforts, the company learned that most retailer systems for merchandisers and buyers operate in isolation. Worse, no retailer it supplied measured forecast accuracy. Realizing it needed a new approach, the company began to forecast its customers' business and track the accuracy of each retailer's forecast.

The results were excellent. When the company started this journey, inventory was at three turns a year, on-time performance was 55 percent, and manufacturing lead times were 140 days. Two years later, inventory is at six turns a year, and the order fill rate exceeds 95 percent. The company also reduced retail compliance fines by 85 percent and logistics costs by 65 percent.

Strategy No. 2: Developing products that create demand

75 percent of new product launches fail. The reason? Because marketing insight is not translated into products, companies don't know what customers want. An AMR Research study of 485 engineering and product development teams showed 52 percent lack a clear understanding of customer requirements.

This is why innovation is a major factor of the AMR Research Supply Chain Top 25 (detailed in Chapter 1). Being quick to market with profitable, high-demand products is vital, but this is not a stand-alone process. Instead, it's infused into the fabric of all supply chain processes. Our research shows 42 percent of companies lack a common set of internal standards for managing the new product development and introduction (NPDI) process. The demand-driven supply network can help.

P&G introduced 10,000 new items in 2002, with an average time from commercialization to shelf presence of three weeks. The use of active cross-functional teams in new product introductions was a major part of P&G's customer-driven initiative. This consumer products leader also encouraged all employees to accept a vision of 360-degree innovation: innovation from peers, other functional teams, suppliers, and customers.

Strategy No. 3: Channel-driven fulfillment

The replenishment decisions of demand-driven leaders are evaluated continuously based on profitability and product placement goals. The team in charge takes responsibility for the success of new product introductions, total channel inventories, and instock performance at the point of purchase. Supply chain velocity and demand visibility are vital elements, but they vary by channel and type of supply chain. Companies manage total channel activity, not just orders for channel replenishment.

The starting point is determining what should lead an order, which varies by channel and customer. Alignment between this definition and order execution must be clear: the order type, the processing and administration of customer priorities, and the agreement on what can be committed all align with customer-oriented fulfillment strategies. These are equally defined for product excesses and shortages: channel runout strategies in times of excess and managing products in times of short supply.

Available-to-promise and capable-to-promise technologies are popular here. Manufacturers want to tie order promise dates to inventory fulfillment in the distribution network or manufacturing. As contract manufacturing and cross-border shipping create more complex networks, supply variability is rising. Companies increasingly need order-promising technologies.

An executive at a consumer products company recently described how the firm had implemented a complex system for committing in-transit inventories. Unfortunately, it didn't work because the company failed to prioritize customers and match customer priorities with order-processing workflows. Lower priority customers used electronic data interchange (EDI) for orders, which were run nightly in a batch job. These orders were processed first and, as a result, received higher priority on inventory availability despite being lower business priority. Higher priority vendor-managed inventory customer orders were processed later in the day, and product was often out of stock. By changing the process to simultaneously consider the order flow and customer and product priorities, order fulfillment improved three percent.

Strategy No. 4: Demand-driven replenishment

Demand-driven replenishment is the alignment of distribution and manufacturing processes for a pull-based response. The supply network synchronizes global planning with local execution and executes in a pull-based system of replenishment.

Demand-driven replenishment builds on the principles of lean manufacturing—waste reduction and pull-based replenishment—connecting local execution with the global planning processes using pull-based network design and constraint-based planning in S&OP. The difference is that these principles do not stop with manufacturing. They link closely to the management of procurement and logistics decisions in the building of agile networks. Leaders in demand-driven replenishment include HP's digital camera division, Toyota, and Johnson Controls.

Snack food maker Wise Foods sells its goods using a direct store delivery program with a 2.5 day order cycle time. In 2003, the company saw need for a change. Order visibility was minimal, scheduling was manual, and when goods were not in the warehouse, the manufacturing lines were shut down and short-cycled to meet customer demand. The wrong products were often shipped, trucks were frequently shipped less than full, and the warehouse wait times were too long.

Wise turned to a demand-driven replenishment strategy, which, in the words of its SVP of manufacturing and logistics, "had to start with blowing the walls out of the functional silos between logistics and manufacturing. The technology was an enabler, but the organizational and process changes were fundamental."

The company classified the project into three phases: the learning curve, the user comfort zone, and the time for user synergy. The learning curve for the factory schedulers to train and use the product was three months, and the team took an additional six months of learning with the product to get comfortable with it. At the end of nine months, inventory was slashed 30 percent, the order fill rate rose from 98.6 to 99.5 percent, and labor productivity improved 10 percent, with overtime cut 40 percent.

Strategy No. 5: Building agile supply networks for customer-centered replenishment

Agile supply networks align material suppliers, contract manufacturers, and logistics providers to a demand signal. The network, designed for pull-based replenishment, is continually refined through NPDI processes. Outsourced manufacturing makes these principles more complex—and more essential.

Based on a recent study of brand owners and contract manufacturers, 54 percent collaborate on the sourcing of materials. Defining multitier inventory replenishment rules and contract strategies based on customer and product priorities is vital.

Agile networks start with design and then flex based on joint agreements. Contract relationships and demand visibility are critical. The key elements of agility and reliability are balanced with cost for the selection of manufacturing sites, supplier qualifications, and modes of transportation.

Successful companies have aligned engineering NPDI processes with shaping networks for a pull-based response. Consider Disney's Buena Vista Home Entertainment, which manages DVD replenishment of new releases with a two-day cycle in a direct shipment model. Actual consumer demand is uncertain, with up to 70 percent of new title sales occurring during the first 10 days of a product release.

Multiple formats (such as 4:3 and 16:9 aspect ratios), customized packaging, and targeted promotional offers for different retailers (the *Shark Tale* DVD is different at Wal-Mart than at Target) further complicate matters.

To handle this complexity, Disney details planning at the store planogram level based on a direct feed of point-of-sale consumption. This plan is then converted to action. A network of six to eight suppliers uses postponement principles to burn DVDs on demand to satisfy the two-day shipment direct to the stores.

A journey of 1,000 miles begins with five steps

These five steps start the demand-driven journey. Before beginning, though, companies must know what it means to be agile and understand the nature of most supply chains.

Supply Chain Chaos
and the Need for Agility

PART
TWO

Terror attacks, port closings, hurricanes, labor strikes, disease outbreaks, and the unknown—these risks discussed in Chapter 5 demand that companies take supply chain agility to the next level. But while everybody understands the importance of supply chain agility, there's little clarity on exactly what it is or how to measure it.

Defining supply chain agility

An agile supply chain senses and responds quickly, easily, predictably, and with high quality.

Speed

Agility requires enough speed to sense routine and unanticipated demand at consumption, and effectively broadcast the signal for an intelligent supply chain response. For example, how long does it take your company—not just your marketing organization, but your supply chain organization—to see true, real-time demand as it's happening in the channel or at your end customer? How long does it then take your supply chain to respond?

Ease

Of course, it's about more than speed. Agility is also about how nimble a company is when things don't go as expected, and how easy it is for a company to sense the change and respond to it.

To get a handle on what ease means in this context, consider the opposite: if a supply chain can quickly sense and respond to a change in demand, but with difficulty, what would it look like in a real-world supply chain? Let's paint a picture: seasoned expediters with allocation rules posted on their cubicle, Post-It notes on every order, and the weekend contact numbers of every carrier and supplier on speed dial. It's the existence of lots of constraints in the master production schedule, and it's evidenced by constant interventions—expediting in sourcing and distribution, manual exception-handling activities, changeovers in production, and more—all of which cost money and time.

Predictability

The response of a supply chain has to be predictable, too. It's no good if you can sometimes sense and respond quickly and easily, but other times you cannot. In fact, predictability can be even more important than absolute speed (assuming that speed remains bounded within a certain time frame). A company that can respond quickly and easily in three days every time is a more desirable company to do business with than one that sometimes responds in a day, but other times takes six.

Quality

There has to be high quality. A supply chain that senses and responds quickly, easily, and predictably, but with poor quality orders and/or product, is not agile.

No one can have just one

An agile supply chain can withstand disruption and displays resiliency or buoyancy in the face of uncertainty and massive variability. But it's not just one supply chain—for most companies, it's many. In a recent AMR Research survey, 27 percent of manufacturers said they have more than 10 supply chains, with 15 percent having 5 to 10 and 37 percent having 2 to 4. Only 20 percent said they had only one. As supply chain management becomes more complex, characterizing and modeling your supply chains become increasingly important.

Supply chain complexity has increased, and products and channels are more diverse. For many manufacturers, this is an "ah-ha" moment, which leads to the next question: how to best categorize supply chains. Unfortunately, there is no one formula.

Each supply chain has its own rhythm that needs to be modeled and refined for optimum response. It's much like raising children: each child requires a different approach that is based on experimentation and discovery. Likewise, each supply chain needs the right mix of pull and push based on agility, inventory strategies, and perceived supply risk.

How do you categorize your supply chains?
10 questions to answer

To help you categorize your supply chains while providing a matrix for improving agility, answer the following questions:

1. Is your supply chain lean or fat?
2. Is your supply chain quick or slow?
3. Does your supply chain have predictable or unpredictable demand?
4. Are you supplying simple or highly complex products?
5. Do you face reliable or unreliable supply conditions?
6. Is your supply chain long or short?
7. Is your supply chain supported by heavily promoted marketing dollars, or is it not promoted?
8. Are you focusing on fashion items or basic products?
9. Is product based on complex distribution networks, or are distribution systems based on simple networks?
10. Is your supply chain dependent on aftermarket service? If so, to what degree?

Develop a spreadsheet using these descriptors, and map products to these characteristics to redesign supply chains. Look for patterns and define supply chains based on having similar characteristics.

For supply chains that are lean and long, need to be quick, behave like fashion supply chains, or have unpredictable demand and supply in highly complex environments, designing for agility is critical. Using the principles of agility outlined above, this supply response is predictable despite demand variation.

The following metrics provide a measure for supply chain agility.

Speed and predictability

A measure of end-to-end cycle time—made up of the sequential sourcing, manufacturing, order/demand processing, and delivery/distribution cycle times—can be used to capture speed and predictability. The mean or median cycle times describe how quickly the supply chain responds. The range and standard deviation of the cycle times reveal how predictable the speed of response is and, therefore, how predictable the process is. A company that has a mean manufacturing cycle time of 15 days, but a standard deviation of +/- 13 days, clearly has an unpredictable manufacturing process, one with potentially high levels of rework and poor Right First Time performance.

Ease

The major impediments to ease and flexibility are complexity and too many constraints. One possibility is to measure the constraints at each point in the supply chain: for example, the number of labor, material, or capacity constraints in the master production schedule, the amount of fixed planning time (such as the length of the S&OP process), the extent to which the product and manufacturing process design allows a postponement strategy, and others.

Another possibility is to measure the result of a "hard" process. As noted earlier, if it's hard, there are constant interventions—expediting, schedule disruptions, and changeovers—that show up in your costs. As such, cost can be a good indicator of the ease with which the supply chain responds. In conjunction with the other metrics, a clear measure of the variability of total supply chain costs will help ensure that supply chain response is truly agile.

A third possibility, which combines the two above, is to look at a ratio of variable to fixed costs. Fixed costs represent constraints. A relatively higher ratio of variable to fixed costs indicates greater flexibility in changing an organization's operations to meet unexpected changes in demand or supply.

Quality

Here you can look at measures of quality at each major point in the supply chain: supplier quality, manufacturing quality, and quality of the order (and product) delivered to the customer.

The real test comes when you compare these variables to demand forecast error by product category and channel. If a company can respond with a small variance to a forecast that has high variability, its supply chain is responding quickly and predictably in the face of variable demand. If it can combine that with reasonable costs and high quality, it has the makings of an agile supply chain.

Becoming agile

Four metric categories taken together show a company's supply chain agility:

- **Cycle times**—Median and variance around a mean—to measure speed and predictability
- **Cost**—As a proxy to measure the ease with which the supply chain responds
- **Quality**—Supplier, manufacturing, and order/product—to describe the quality of the outcome at each major point in the supply chain
- **Demand forecast error**—To measure the variability of demand a company faces

Agility doesn't just happen. It has to be designed using network design systems, refined using inventory configuration, and implemented with a redefinition of what is important in operations management. Table 1 outlines 25 agility factors to consider in your supply chain redesign.

Factor	Design	Deliver	Make	Source
Cost	Improve transparency between procurement and R&D	Implement demand visibility systems for quick response	Reduce cycle times	Focus on raw and semifinished goods inventories
	Make direct material requirements visible early in stage-gate process	Reduce demand error	Reduce changeovers and improve labor flexibility	Implement systems for demand-driven supply management
			Improve the ration of variable/fixed costs	
Quality	Improve quality of design	Reduce warehouse complexity through SKU rationalization	Focus on manufacturing reliability; products are Right First Time	Focus on supplier reliability: supplier development and Six Sigma programs with suppliers
		Use vendor-managed inventory programs		
Time	Improve platform reuse and simplify global formulations	Deploy warehouse postponement strategies	Deploy manufacturing postponement strategies	Make use of design for supply
	Provide alternate bill of materials and suppliers	Implement inventory optimization technologies	Design manufacturing work cells for flexibility	Use supplier-managed inventory programs
		Pool with merge in transit of lumpy demand items		Reduce inbound variability
		Reduce outbound variability		

Table 1: 25 levers to improve agility

Staying agile

The agility of a company's supply chain changes over time as business changes are introduced, whether it's new products, outsourcing, or new distribution channel constraints. A company's supply chain agility is elastic, even at one point in time. It may be agile enough to respond effectively to a 10 percent uptick in demand, for example, but not a 20 percent uptick.

Companies should, therefore, test for supply chain agility on a regular basis. Just as organizations perform periodic drills to test their emergency responses—fire, hurricane, earthquake, and flood—they should practice annual or biannual agility drills using simulation software. These tests should be grounded in reality (for example, 200 percent over-subscribed on a new product or loss of a major channel) and conducted in periodic intervals to assess organizational ability and a profitable response to demand fluctuations. The simulation should highlight at what point a company is no longer able to respond quickly and cost effectively given its current product design, sourcing options, manufacturing and warehouse facility network design, and distribution network design, and what would happen if any of these were changed.

Measuring agility, however, isn't all that needs to be done. First, overall supply chain health needs to be diagnosed. It's an ongoing process that is vital to the ideals of being demand driven.

Diagnosing Your Supply Chain Health With the Metrics that Matter

A map for the demand-driven journey is the first step to assessing the health of the supply chain. AMR Research's benchmarking team has found that companies can quickly assess their supply chain health using just three key metrics: demand forecast accuracy, perfect order fulfillment, and supply chain cost.

Effective performance measurement remains difficult

One of the vital ingredients for carrying out renewable, strategic business change is ongoing performance measurement. Measuring supply chain performance is not a new practice. Most companies measure at least some aspect of their supply chain and understand the need for a more comprehensive measurement program, yet measuring performance remains difficult. Why? Two reasons, mainly:

- **An abundance of possibilities**—Figuring out what to measure to yield the most information and benefit from the least investment of resources is one major hurdle. The problem is not a lack of possible metrics, but an overwhelming number of choices.
- **Enablers add to the complexity**—While traditional measurement focuses solely on operational performance indicators such as cycle times and inventory levels, companies also need to bring into the equation the application technologies and best practices that facilitate performance. Benchmarking these is critical to having actionable information; they go beyond the question of how a company is doing to why: *Why are we at our current performance levels? What effect are our technologies and best practices having on our performance? What are the best-in-class companies doing differently than we are?*

Interdependencies among metrics

The goal: focusing on the few critical metrics that really matter—the ones that provide the most balanced view of end-to-end supply chain performance, allowing companies to see how they're doing and where they're making tradeoffs.

Before identifying these most important metrics, you must understand how all the possible supply chain metrics interrelate. The metrics reflect the underlying realities of the supply chain they measure. As such, none exist in a vacuum, although this is often how they're treated.

Consider the typical interdependencies we see in our benchmarking studies. To illustrate these relationships, we compare two companies: Company A and Company B.

Trading off high inventories for good order quality

Compared to its peers, Company A has high inventories, long cash-to-cash cycle time, good order quality (as seen in its perfect order metric), and low demand forecast accuracy. What's going on? Low demand forecast accuracy indicates that Company A has poor visibility into demand. But the company still wants to be able to give its customers what they want, when they want it. So what does it do? It makes extra finished goods, keeping an inventory buffer to avoid stockouts. High inventories, in turn, create a longer end-to-end cash cycle time as well as a good perfect order performance. Company A is willing to pay the price of high inventory holding costs so it can maintain good customer responsiveness levels.

Sacrificing customer responsiveness for low costs

Company B, on the other hand, has low inventories, short cash-to-cash cycle time, poor order quality, and low demand forecast accuracy. This company is clearly more concerned with maintaining margins than customer responsiveness. It also has low demand forecast accuracy, but it's keeping inventories lean and cash cycle times short. The result: high stockouts lead to poor perfect order performance. The tradeoff: Company B is sacrificing customer responsiveness for a strong cost structure.

Note the pattern here: demand visibility affecting inventories, cash cycle times, and perfect order fulfillment. While there are clearly more interdependencies and scenarios, this pattern of interaction holds in every company, albeit with different specifics.

See Table 2 for supply chain metric definitions.

The importance of demand visibility

For both of these companies, demand visibility is at the heart of their issues. This is supported by analysis of our benchmarking data, which shows a strong correlation between demand forecast accuracy and perfect order fulfillment across industry. Companies with good demand visibility have better perfect order performance, and companies with poor demand visibility have worse perfect order performance (see Figure 1). At best, poor demand visibility forces companies to make tradeoffs between cost and customer responsiveness.

At worst, it fosters poor performance in both cost and responsiveness.

Metric	Definition
Perfect order	An order that is complete, accurate, on time, and in perfect condition. Two conditions prevent a perfect order: —Orders not delivered on time because of stockout/ manufacturing delay, late shipment, or in-transit/ delivery delays —Order not meeting customer requirements because of inaccurate shipment, poor quality of finished goods, or damage to finished goods in transit
Demand forecast accuracy	The difference between forecasted and actual demand. Specifically, this is the inverse of the mean absolute percent error between forecasted and actual demand.
Cash-to-cash cycle time	The length of time between when a company spends cash to buy raw materials to the time cash flows back into the company from its customers. It includes the following metrics: —Ship to customer delivery (time taken from shipment of finished goods to delivery at customer's address) —Raw material receipt to payment (time from receipt of raw materials to payment; also called days payables outstanding) —Inventory days (average days of inventory on hand) —Days sales outstanding (measurement of the average collection period from invoicing to cash receipt)
Supply chain management cost	Includes direct purchasing operating cost, manufacturing operating cost, transportation cost, warehouse/distribution center operating cost, inventory holding cost, and customer service operating cost.

Table 2: Supply chain metrics definitions

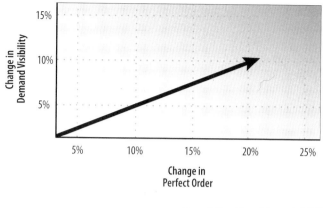

Figure 1: The effect of demand visibility

Introducing the hierarchy of supply chain metrics

While demand forecast, costs, and order quality are clearly important indicators of overall performance, effective action takes additional metrics. But what metrics? Indiscriminately adding metrics into the pot is not the answer. What's needed is a multilevel approach that allows an increasingly deeper focus. AMR Research's solution is the hierarchy of supply chain metrics, which defines a tiered system of metrics to improve supply chain effectiveness. The top tier assesses a company's supply chain health, and the two successive tiers diagnose the root cause of performance gaps and provide insight for corrective action.

Each tier serves a different purpose that is aimed at a different goal (see Figure 2):

· **Top tier: Supply chain health assessment**—This is the 50,000-foot level, at which an executive can assess, with just three metrics, the overall health of the supply chain and the high-level tradeoffs a company might be making.

· **Mid level: Supply chain diagnostic**—The next level of detail is the 25,000-foot view. This level uses a composite cash flow metric to provide an initial diagnostic tool.

· **Ground level: Supply chain effectiveness**—The bottom level uses a variety of metrics that supports effective root cause analysis and allows surgical, highly efficient corrective action.

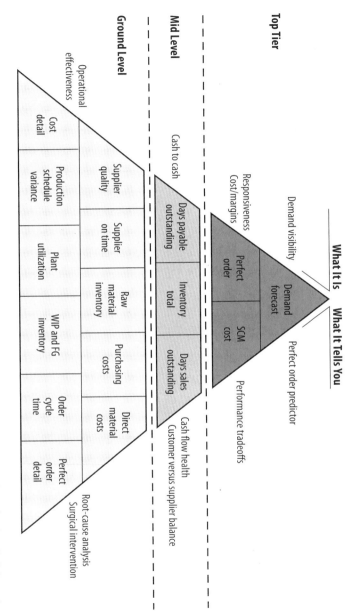

Figure 2: The hierarchy of supply chain metrics

Top tier: supply chain health assessment

At the highest level of the hierarchy are three key metrics: demand forecast accuracy, perfect order fulfillment, and supply chain management total cost (refer back to Table 1). As demonstrated earlier, demand forecast accuracy has predictive power: the extent of a company's demand visibility can predict the responsiveness of its supply chain, as evidenced by its perfect order rating.

Of course, responsiveness by itself does not guarantee a healthy supply chain. Companies have gone out of business while they're being responsive because they lost sight of costs. What's essential is to look at the balance between perfect order fulfillment and supply chain management cost. Most companies make a tradeoff between two performance areas: customer responsiveness, as captured in their perfect order fulfillment rating, and costs.

Mid level: supply chain diagnostic

The next level of the hierarchy looks beyond overall customer responsiveness and cost to the cash-to-cash metric—how well is your company managing its cash flow? Are there immediate opportunities to take some cash off the table?

The cash-to-cash metric is a composite that includes customer and supplier payment times and total inventories. It allows a company to see whether the time it takes to pay its suppliers and the time it takes a company's customers to pay are in balance. This metric determines whether the bellwether inventory metric, which can contribute to high cost and/or a low perfect order, deserves further analysis. High inventories might be a result of excess in any of the components of raw materials, work in process (WIP), or finished goods (FG). Each is a symptom of a different underlying problem.

Ground level: supply chain effectiveness

Analysis of the detailed metrics on the ground level of the hierarchy allows a company to identify and implement the specific interventions that address the root cause of issues identified at the first two levels with the most efficient and targeted use of resources. In our benchmarking research, we have a portfolio of approximately 45 operational metrics, some of which are listed in Figure 2.

Metrics at the ground level include supplier effectiveness indicators, such as the percentage of supplier receipts that passed quality and on-time standards and the raw material inventories, purchasing operating costs, and direct material costs that are often affected by and interact with supplier performance. Also included here are metrics that indicate a company's level of operational effectiveness, including further supply chain management cost details, production schedule variance, plant utilization, WIP and FG inventories, order cycle time, and details about the perfect order fulfillment total.

Using the hierarchy of supply chain metrics— a case example

Consider the example of ConsumerCo, a $1 billion manufacturer of household products that has kept its costs low to support its overall business strategy of being a lower cost provider than its competitors while keeping product quality on par with the market. It now has some specific opportunities to shore up its external relationships—with suppliers, logistics providers, and customers—in targeted ways. By doing so, ConsumerCo can continue to keep costs down while improving its customer responsiveness.

Top tier: trading off customer responsiveness for cost

At the top tier of the hierarchy, ConsumerCo's demand forecast accuracy is low, its perfect order rating is on the low side at 5 percent below the average, and its supply chain management total costs are good. Consistent with its strategy, the company is reining in costs, but doing so at the expense of customer responsiveness.

Mid level: high inventories and a cash management opportunity

ConsumerCo's overall cash cycle time is slightly longer than the average, but not worrisome. However, the component metrics are more interesting.

High inventories

Given that its perfect order rating is low (though it's not yet apparent why), it's likely that the problem with the perfect order

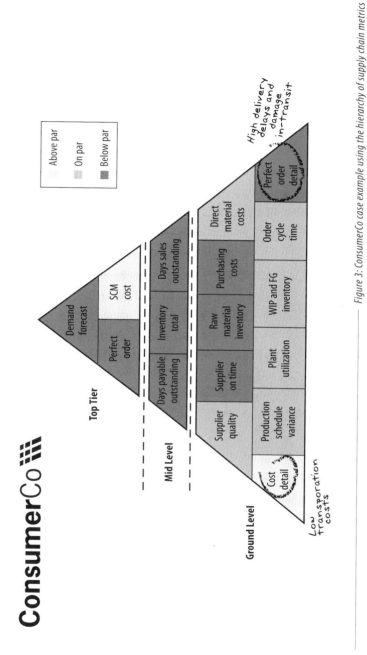

Figure 3: ConsumerCo case example using the hierarchy of supply chain metrics

is not a lack of inventory. However, it might still be the case that ConsumerCo has the wrong inventory or lacks visibility into its inventory.

Cash management opportunities

ConsumerCo pays its suppliers in 30 days on average, but its customers take an average of 43 days to pay it. This points to some immediate cash flow opportunities. Also, the long days sales outstanding might be related to poor perfect order performance, reflecting customer dissatisfaction with order quality.

Ground level: supplier performance, logistics execution, and customer payment times

A deeper root cause analysis uncovers specific supplier, logistics provider, and customer areas in which to target corrective action.

Supplier relationships

While finished goods inventories are slightly high, the real culprit is 20 percent higher than average raw material inventory. At the same time, the supplier on-time rating (the rate at which suppliers meet on-time commitments of raw material) is 5 percent lower than the average, a likely contributor to higher raw materials that serve as a buffer. An examination of the costs that relate to suppliers reveals slightly high purchasing operating costs and on par direct material costs. In a nutshell, ConsumerCo is paying its suppliers well and, as exposed in the cash-to-cash metric, paying them relatively quickly, but it is not receiving the service levels it requires from its suppliers.

Logistics provider relationships

The components of the perfect order uncover the source of the low perfect order rating. Rather than stockouts or inaccurate ship-ments (which would point to inventory problems), it's delivery delays and damage in transit that are the culprits here, each 10 percent higher than average. Since both of these relate to a transportation theme, we look at the related cost details. Consistent with its low total supply chain management costs, ConsumerCo's transportation costs are very good, at 4 percent below the average. One possibility is that it might be paying its logistics providers so far below industry standards that service levels suffer. ConsumerCo should reconsider pricing and service-level agreements with its logistics providers.

Customer relationships

Corrective action that improves the perfect order might also help improve customer payment times, thus improving overall cash cycle time. As with demand forecast accuracy at the top tier, ConsumerCo also has an opportunity to work more closely with its customers to improve demand visibility.

Enabler information provides basis for corrective action

Once you've assessed and diagnosed the health of your supply chain using the hierarchy, specific corrective actions can be identified. This is where a solid understanding of where you stand with regard to using application technology and best practices becomes critical, since these serve as important levers to help adjust performance.

In the case of ConsumerCo, besides possibly revisiting the agreements it has with its suppliers and logistics providers, it can examine its supplier and logistics provider-related technology and practices. To what extent is it sharing forecasts with its suppliers and logistics providers? Is it using electronic connections to speed up purchase orders to suppliers and tenders to logistics providers? Similarly with its customer relationships, are customers sharing forecasts with ConsumerCo to the extent possible to help demand visibility? How does ConsumerCo's use of technology and processes compare to that of its peers and, in particular, to the best-performing companies?

Taking action

Measuring performance is a critical underpinning of a well-run business. The hierarchy of supply chain metrics contains the right level of the right metrics and provides a structured approach to continuous, effective, and efficient performance measurement and improvement. The operational performance metrics contained in the hierarchy should be supplemented by an accurate measure of a company's use of technology and processes to help determine the most effective corrective action to take.

Companies should use the hierarchy of supply chain metrics to do the following:

· **Track performance on an ongoing basis**. Measure at regular intervals so you can track performance changes. It's particularly useful to have baselined your performance prior to a major market or organizational change (such as implementation of a new system) to get a clear picture of the effect of the change on performance.

· **Put a structured evaluation program in place**. Implement a structured process to evaluate, analyze, and act on the results of the measurement. Many companies have key performance indicators in place that they measure, but the results sit on a shelf collecting dust.

· **Work with trading partners**. Rather than simply shifting costs and responsibilities around the supply network, work with trading partners—customers, suppliers, and logistics providers—to drive costs out of the supply chain and improve end-customer responsiveness across the network.

Acronyms and Initialisms

A&D	Aerospace and defense	OECD	Organization for Economic Co-operation and Development
ACE	Automated Commercial Environment		
ATDI	Advanced Trade Data Initiative	OEM	Original equipment manufacturer
C-TPAT	Customs-Trade Partnership Against Terrorism	PAT	Process Analytical Technology
CAD	Computer-aided design	PLM	Product lifecycle management
CAGR	Compound annual growth rate	R&D	Research and Development
CDC	Centers for Disease Control	RDB	Relational database
DDSN	Demand-driven supply network	REACH	Registration, Evaluation, and Authorization of Chemicals
EDI	Electronic data interchange		
ELV	End-of-Life Vehicles	RFID	Radio frequency identification
EMEA	Europe, Middle East, and Africa	ROA	Return on assets
EPA	Environmental Protection Agency	RoHS	Restriction of Hazardous Substances
ERP	Enterprise resource planning	S&OP	Sales and operations planning
ETI	Ethical Trading Initiative	SOX	Sarbanes-Oxley Act
EU	European Union	SCM	Supply chain management
FDA	Food and Drug Administration	SEC	Securities and Exchange Commission
FG	Finished goods		
GDP	Gross domestic product	SKU	Stock-keeping unit
GRI	Global Reporting Initiative	UNDP	United Nations Development Programme
IND	Investigational new drug		
IP	Intellectual property	VC	Venture capital
IT	Information technology	WEEE	Waste Electrical and Electronic Equipment
NPDI	New product development and introduction		
		WIP	Work in process

Index

A

A&D companies
  RoHS compliance, 98
  supplier failure and risk
    management, 145–146
Abbott, 122, 127
Active compliance framework, 81–87
Advanced Trade Data Initiative
  (ATDI), 160
Africa
  pharmaceutical companies and
    AIDS, 124–127
Agility, supply chain
  build agile supply networks
    for customer-centered
    replenishment, 169–170
  categorizing supply chain, 174
  compared to risk management,
    150
  defining characteristics, 171–173
  factors for becoming, 176–177
  metrics for measuring, 176–177
  network design for and risk
    management, 157
  speed, ease, predictability, and
    quality, 171–173, 175–176
  staying, 178
AIDS
  pharmaceutical companies
    in Africa and, 124–127
American Eagle, 107

Anheuser-Busch
  as Supply Chain Top 25, 22
Anticipating stage of demand-
  driven maturity, 15–16, 46–47
AstraZeneca, 119, 124
Automated Commercial
  Environment (ACE), 159–160
Avian flu. *See Pandemic (avian flu)*

B

B&Q, 109
Bär, Hans J., 20
Baxter, 133
Bayer, 122
Beijing, 57
Best Buy
  as Supply Chain Top 25, 22
Bill and Melinda Gates Foundation,
  127
BioCryst Pharmaceuticals, 133
BMW, 92
Boston Scientific, 121–122
Brand risk, 151
Bullwhip effect, 8
Business process management
  environmental compliance, 83
Buy-side contract management, 158

C

Capacity risk, 151

193

ground level: supply chain
effectiveness, 183–186
hierarchy overview, 183–186
importance of demand visibility, 181
interdependencies among, 180–181
for measuring agility, 175–176
mid level: supply chain diagnostic,
183–185
perfect order, 182
supply chain management cost, 182
taking action, 190
top tier: supply chain health
assessment, 183–185
Metro Group, 104
Mid level: supply chain diagnostic,
183–185
Moment of truth, 6
healthcare and, 117
organizational redesign and, 49
Motorola
as Supply Chain Top 25, 22

N

Natural disasters
Hurricane Katrina as risk
management example, 152–153
supply chain, ix, xi, xiii
Nayar, Nandkumar, 20
Nestle, 43
Networks
create value networks, 44
in demand-driven supply
networks, 6–7

designing for agility, 157
New product development and
introduction (NPDI) process, 167
building agile networks for
customer-centered
replenishment, 169–170
New products. *See Product innovation*
Nike, 20, 93, 104, 110
cheap labor and, 39
corporate responsibility, 40
recycling product program, 105
as Supply Chain Top 25, 23
Nissan
honorable mention for Supply
Chain Top 25, 25
Nokia, 19
as Supply Chain Top 25, 21
Novartis, 43, 120, 124

O

Office Depot
electronics recycling program,
104–105
Oil Purification Systems, 106
Operating strategies
create value networks, 44
involve cross-functional teams in
joint value creation, 44
realize right IT infrastructure
makes a difference, 45
recognize need for improved demand
and supply visibility signals, 45
S&OP processes to execute global
business strategies, 44

United Nations Millennium
Development Goal, 38
UPS, 106

V

Vaccines, 132–133
Value creation
create value networks, 44
geographic hubs and, 48
involve cross-functional teams in
joint value creation, 44
Value networks
creating, 44

W

Wal-Mart, xi, 20, 30, 134, 152
as Supply Chain Top 25, 21
Warfare
supply chain and, xiii
Waste Electrical and Electronic
Equipment (WEEE), 93
cost of compliance, 70
deadline for, 96
logistics nightmare of, 99
overview of, 67–69
Whiskering, 96
White goods
RoHS compliance, 98
Whole Foods, 107, 152
Wise Foods
demand-driven replenishment,
169
Woodcock, Janet, 119

Woolworths
as Supply Chain Top 25, 22
World hunger
supply chain and, vii, xiii
Wyeth, 120

Contributors

The following people contributed to the content of this book:
Greg Aimi, Mike Burkett, Lora Cecere, John Davies, Rob Garf,
John Hagerty, Mark Hillman, Debra Hofman, Eric Karofsky,
Heather Keltz, Roddy Martin, Hussain Mooraj, Mickey North Rizza,
and Joe Souza.

About AMR Research

Research and Advice That Matter

AMR Research is the No. 1 advisory firm focused on the intersection of business process with supply chain and ERP. Founded in 1986, we provide subscription advisory services and peer networking opportunities to operations and IT executives in the consumer products, life sciences, manufacturing, and retail sectors.

Since 1995, we have published over 14,000 pieces of research. Our analysts focus on delivering independent, leading-edge research on both established and emerging technologies. This analysis is supported by daily interaction with the most extensive network of market contacts and the best quantitative data in the industry.

125 Summer Street
Fourth Floor
Boston, MA 02110
Tel: +1-617-542-6600
Fax: +1-617-542-5670

555 Montgomery Street
Suite 650
San Francisco, CA 94111
Tel: +1-415-217-3737

Parkshot House
5 Kew Road
Richmond, Surrey
TW9 2PR
United Kingdom
Tel: +44 (0) 20 8334 8090
Fax: +44 (0) 20 8334 8190

Colophon

Supply Chain Saves the World is printed on Synergy Natural 100PCW from SMART Papers. This paper is completely manufactured from post-consumer fiber. The cover contains no recycled content.

The body text and table typeface is Filosofia from Emigre. The figures feature Myriad Pro, originally designed by Robert Slimbach and Carol Twombly.

The original design of this book is by Jason Warriner (www.jaywar.com).

Angela Tavares, Joseph Neylon, Jason Leary, and Mike Brown did the proofreading, layout, and production work.